Quartet

four-part harmony
from a recollected life

Judith Ren-Lay

Quartet

*four-part harmony
from a recollected life*

Quartet
four-part harmony from a recollected life
Judith Ren-Lay

Copyright © 2022 Judith Ren-Lay

ISBN 978-1-7372036-1-2

Library of Congress Control Number: 2022917639

FIRST EDITION

Front and Back Cover design by Noah Diamond
Interior Design by Judith Ren-Lay

Published by Vaudevisuals Press

Author website: http://www.judithren-lay.com
Publisher website: http://www.vvpress.com

BISAC categories:
B10001000 Biography & Autobiography / Artists, Architects, Photographers
BIO026000 Biography & Autobiography / Personal Memoirs
BIO005000 Biography & Autobiography / Entertainment & Performing Arts

1.

Dedicated
to friends and peers
who brought support and encouragement
to this unlikely life.

CONTENTS

2.

Preface

I survived the 2021 pandemic months largely by pulling forty years of writing and photographs together and sending (in the form of pdf books) to an email list of 200 friends who had agreed to be recipients. Thanks to all these dear readers for giving me the strength to keep at it. Created as a series, this autobiographical material reveals facets of a life from four very different perspectives – origins, work, thought, challenge. When considering the chance to have it published the only clear way to go was to combine the four into one. Life is, after all, perceived through changing perspectives.

I. Soprano

3.

A Life Revisited
early life from birth to 32

A Life Revisited

Born Judith Ren Lay in Denver, Colorado on January 15, 1943. Father Willard Vernell Lay, drafted into the Navy as a Yeoman typed his way through WWII. Mother Earlene Vilna Haas, daughter of Myrtle Alexander Haas and Earle Cleveland Haas, the doctor who invented Tampax. One sister, Merlyn Diane Lay, four years older. These 5 people formed the central core of family. There were a couple of aunts and uncles who cycled in and out of closeness – Daddy's sister Ren (after whom I was named who partnered with a woman named Faye all their lives) and his brother Harry Lay, married to Cleda, no children. Mother had one brother Ted Haas, married to Vera and they had two daughters Carol and Dorothy. They are all gone with the exception of several 2nd cousins long out of touch.

They live in memory and remain part of me.

As early as I can remember I was listening to Barber Shop quartets. Both my father and uncle participated. Daddy taught himself to play piano by ear. I took lessons and had a bit of a gift, but couldn't invest myself, being too easily distracted with Girl Scouts, social activities and school. As a young teen I taught vacation bible school and sang in the choir at Bonnie Brae Baptist Church where my parents met and were founding members. The family rarely went to church, but my father faithfully printed the weekly church bulletin. I had classmates who were Episcopalian and attended camp with them, becoming fascinated with apostolic succession. Religion was simply a given, not a calling, as it afforded me access to interesting music and an expanded social network. My sister and I were rarely disciplined, as all socialization was encouraged and study of anything deemed not as important. My sister got pregnant in high school and my doctor grandfather gave her an abortion at home.

Early influence of religion, music, girl scouts, having a social life, and little parental supervision or interference.

My sister and I were taught that our purpose was to find a decent man to marry who could make a good living. Working at various jobs for money was expected before that happened. I started working at 13 as a candy girl at the Mayan movie theater, managed by a family friend, then moved up to cashier when I got a little older. My father at that time was working as a booker for United Artists. His job was to book films into Denver theaters. As a result we were members of an organization called Variety Club International, centered on the entertainment industry. Every Thursday night was family night and we all went to the club for dinner and then upstairs to the screening room where we saw a film that had not yet been released. The dynamic of movies captured my imagination. In junior high school I even wrote an autobiography titled *Hollywood Here I Come.*

It was a circuitous route, never ending up in Hollywood.
Instead I landed in New York after two marriages.

My high school boyfriend was an intellectual and an outsider who drove a 1949 baby blue Oldsmobile. He was a year ahead of me in school and worlds ahead in reading, being heavily into James Joyce. I only went to college because I wanted to be with him.

Putting finding that partner ahead of any consideration
of my own direction alone.

All through high school and two years of college I had a job at Sears and Roebuck in ladies ready-to-wear, working two nights a week and weekends through high school. When I moved to Boulder to attend the University of Colorado, I also worked at Sears over Christmas, Spring and Summer vacations. During college I was cashier at the University Cafeteria, never knowing what it was like to not have a job. Earning my own money was a given, since family resources were always short.

I was responsible for all expenses except the minimum
state college tuition which my parents managed.
Everything I ever wanted was a problem to obtain until
I began working for my own money at 13. After that,
and for the rest of my life it was a matter of piecing
together jobs to cover expenses, never able to save or get
ahead of the game. Month to month has been the way I
have lived for 8 decades.

In Boulder I was rushed by Delta Gamma and pledged, soon realizing Greek life was not for me, after landing a role in the Drama School production of *Ah Wilderness!* playing Nora, the maid. I hungrily embraced the theater. Introduced to a free spirited life of aspiring young actors, I threw off many of the strictures in which I had been raised to believe. I was fascinated to learn about gay culture for the first time and hung out with a loyal group of like-minded folks, a core of inseparables in the early 60's who competed with each another, lived with each other, appeared in productions with each another and learned from each other. It was just before the great sexual revolution. Somehow I managed to remain a virgin.

> *My own sexual epiphany was delayed until 1975 when I moved to New York.*

Thomas William Fowler Osburn, an older member of that CU theater club returned to Boulder for graduate work and to appear in the summer Shakespeare Festival the same year I won a scholarship for the summer musical *The King & I.* Our paths crossed and he took me over. That was the summer I became a dancer. I had auditioned for *Romeo & Juliet* and the director wanted to cast me as Juliet, but the director of the musical claimed me (because of the scholarship) to play Eliza and so that summer, instead of Shakespeare, I was dancing the lead role in the *Small House of Uncle Thomas* ballet. Our courtship continued through the fall and we eloped to his parent's home in Houston over Thanksgiving. I left college in my junior year jumping out of the frying pan into the fire with a man of 29 when I had just turned 19.

> *Easily wooed by those I believed stronger, more intelligent and talented than me. Always instinctively attached to the theater.*

Turned out he was a closet homosexual and practicing alcoholic, who never could follow through on anything. Being highly paranoid he kept me removed from friends and family and created an aura of mayhem wherever we went. We moved many times first to Texas where we lived on his parents ranch, then Appomattox, Virginia where he started a pipe-line engineering job and eventually to

Spartanburg, South Carolina and New Haven, Connecticut where he obtained teaching jobs in private schools.

Attracted to anti-social behavior and solving other people's problems. I got out of that marriage quickly when I began attending al-anon meetings and realized most of the other wives there were Roman Catholic and didn't believe in divorce. That was not a problem for me. My family supported me in this as they never liked him to begin with.

With every move I learned skills and worked jobs and finally found out enough of who I was without him to garner the strength to leave. I went to Mexico for a divorce and moved into my own apartment. I was 26. The first tool I bought in my new life was a portable typewriter. I had begun modern dance training with Ernestine Stodelle in New Haven and she hired me for the summer to live with her, her husband John Chamberlain, the Conservative columnist, and their 12 year old boy Johnny. My job was to care for Johnny while she wrote her book on Martha Graham. Her best friend was Anne Morrow Lindbergh, wife of Charles. So I became a live-in nanny and continued my dance training with this venerable beauty who had danced with Jose Limon in Doris Humphrey's company in the early days.

I always loved to dance. Training was another story, as I never learned how to learn well, remaining autodidactic to a fault.

Wanting to complete my degree I then enrolled at the University of Maryland in College Park majoring in Theater, minoring in Dance (one of the only Dance programs at that time not part of a physical education department). It was run by Dorothy Madden and I became her office assistant. Never knowing life without working, I also took a waitress job at a pizza restaurant. During that year I rented an attic room in the house of a woman who was a social worker. I had kept my car, a red Kharman Ghia and traveled back to New Haven throughout the year to visit Richard Galligan, the man I had been seeing after leaving Fowler.

I resisted the Academy, never really enjoyed group effort
or joining in a prescribed way of doing things.

After only one year and still without a degree, I returned to Connecticut and married Richard, picking up my dance training with Ernestine and teaching dance at Community Centers and schools in New Haven. I choreographed for a cooperative company called *The New Haven Dance Ensemble* and for the *Connecticut Ballet* under the direction of Robert Vickery. I was awarded grants for state-wide workshops and eventually rented my own studio and taught classes to all ages, traveling into New York City frequently to study.

Still believed that a partner was the ultimate answer,
but this time I had figured out what I wanted to do with
my life and proceeded to make it happen.

In 1975, at the age of 32, as that marriage was ending, JoAnn Jansen, Katherine Gallagher and I sublet an apartment in New York City on Mott Street between Spring and Prince. That first summer we were 3 wives leaving husbands looking to develop dance careers beyond teaching. One of my students from New Haven was living in the city and her room-mate was Gerry Doff, who became our New York city guide. He had appeared in an early production of *Hair* and was exploring his sexuality at the time. Much later he was one of my first friends to die of AIDS.

We were wild and experimented with sex & drugs, but
always with dance as the central core of our discoveries.
Katherine eventually gave up dance and went into
computers. JoAnn moved to Hollywood and created an
established career in film choreography and coaching. I
just continued to deepen my involvement in performance
and art despite repeated financial ane health challenges.

And so began my New York city journey through dance, performance installation, script, poetry, music, and all the people and places, travels and challenges that accompanied me. I simply exploded with a body, voice and point of view that was undeniable. 46 years later after a heart crisis, a leg crisis and being run down by a taxi, deniability raises its head. I am struggling to know what choices to make going forward as I re-witness and attempt to organize and validate what has been created in all these years with this improbable life.

> *I meet the moment with an organized mind believing that to tell my story is why I was given life. I struggle to also believe this journey is a unique one and deserving of attention in the face of the crowds of loudly visible voices demanding to be heard today.*

At the age of 79, a need for focus prompts this overview of what has passed. Each life contains seeds of many stories as we consider all the various aspects and interpretations our lives present. Ultimately it's what we have to give, whatever it may mean.

Judith Ren-Lay
New York City
June 2022

4. Studio Portrait 2022 j.r-l.

II. Alto

5. from WARRIOR HOSTESS 1986 (photo Jud Hart)

Aesthetic
Practicalities
forty years making art

CONTENTS

~~~~~~~~~~~~~~~~~~

Musings

Of the life and the work. Of the survival, sometimes under unexpected umbrellas. Of how close and how real and how far it goes towards being the same – or a re-enactment of something happening to make it happen. Of more than one time doing it and of being well fed under the strain. Of a way of bringing others into the wave of its motion and sifting variations of discovery. Voices filter through a saturation of stimulation, demonstrating ways. Impulses and frightened necessities curl out. Self-importance is replaced by only a fleeting crumbling need to occasionally demonstrate. Seeking a rather oblique angle with warm reminders. There are ongoing chemical surges in the system, moving with regularity and intensity; the playing out of emotions. Like furtive poltergeists, they inhabit head and guts, crawling up the spine, digging into shoulder blades with an arresting dynamic.

~~~~~~~~~~~~~~~~~~

6. NEW HAVEN circa 1970 (photo Van Galligan)

Early Forays (1943-1979)

I was always an active kid – loving individual sports like gymnastics and dance. My parents didn't have money for lessons, so I just tried stuff out on my own making use of a large grass yard beside our house. A serious cheerleader, our squad practiced every morning all summer to prepare for our senior year.

My father taught my sister and me to ballroom dance on the living room rug and I loved all the school dances from sock hop to prom. Daddy was also an active member of SPEBSQSA (Society for the Preservation and Enjoyment of Barbershop Quartet Singing in America) and he and his brother were part of a practicing quartet as early as I can remember, rehearsing in my family home. I also sang in our Baptist Church Choir, and my High School Concert Choir, acted in school plays as part of the drama club, often performed pantomime to Broadway show tunes for school shows, most memorably *I Cain't Say No* from Oklahoma, loved doing impressions – Johnny Ray, Buddy Holly, Marilyn Monroe, foreign accents. In short, I was a performer. Whenever I could gather an audience I would attempt to entice them with my naive abilities.

As a green freshman at Colorado University in Boulder I tried out for a production of *Ah Wilderness* by Eugene O'Neill and won the role of Nora, the Swedish maid. The director loved that I made the role my own by having her laugh uncontrollably most of the time she was onstage.

In those college years, between the University Player's Club and the local Nomad Playhouse I played parts in productions of Cole Porter/ Bella Spewack's *Kiss Me Kate* (Lois Lane/Bianca) – G.B. Shaw's *Arms and the Man* (Raina) – Strindberg's *The Father* (Bertha) – Rodgers and Hammerstein's *The King & I* (Eliza) – Lorca's *House of Bernarda Alba* (Maria Josepha).

I then married, took the name Judy Osburn and, by way of a theaterless stint in Texas, moved to South Carolina where I performed in a Converse College production of Shaw's *Pygmalion* (Mrs. Eynsford-Hill) and a Spartanburg Little Theater production of John Van Druten's *Bell, Book and Candle* (Gilliam Holroyd with then husband Fowler Osburn as Shepherd Henderson).

From 1963-1967 Judy Osburn taught physical education and dance at private schools and camps in North and South Carolina and Connecticut taking every opportunity to create concerts for student dancers, often utilizing slide projections on moving bodies. Having had little arts education I was making up my own teaching techniques, allowing the imagination to exercise total exploratory freedom. There was some sort of spirit insisting itself upon me.

When we moved to New Haven CT I was introduced to Ernestine Stodelle and my real dance education began. She was a former member of the Doris Humphrey Dancers, where she partnered Jose Limon and was once married to Russian theater director Theodore Komisarjevsky with whom she had three children. When I met her she was married to conservative columnist John Chamberlain and I was hired the summer after my first divorce to live with them at their home in Cheshire, CT and take care of her then 12 year old son Johnny while she wrote her book on Graham, later published as *Deep Song: The Dance Story of Martha Graham.* Ernestine became my artistic mother and through her I first learned in depth about the history and current state of modern dance, modern art and avant-garde music.

I then went back to college for a year at the University of Maryland, and expanded my dance education under the directorship of Dorothy Madden, who had established the very first dance department in the U.S. separate from physical education. At that time I met Kenneth Rinker and Suzette Martinez who became lifelong friends. While there I danced in a production of *Oklahoma* also helping with the choreography. The director wrote me on opening night: "Anything that looks sharp in this production is due largely to your efforts. Those things that may not, I simply failed to have you apply your unfailing touch. Sincere thanks for a job well done."

While I was there, Meredith Monk came to perform in DC at the Smithsonian and I was part of the huge student cast of that 1969 residency. I mainly remember her company dressed in padded suits rolling around the dinosaur installation.

And then I returned to New Haven, remarried, becoming Judith Galligan, and continued my journey, opening a teaching studio, teaching all over Connecticut state under the auspices of the *Connecticut Commission on the Arts*, choreographing for the *Connecticut Ballet* for Robert Vickery, dancing in the companies of Ernestine Stodelle and a cooperative company we called *The New Haven Dance Ensemble* where I choreographed and performed with Sally Hess, Risa Jaroslow, JoAnn Jansen, Katherine Gallagher, Emmy Devine, Ceci Taylor, James Cutting, Elizabeth Kagan, Yvonne Parker, and Jo Linton.

All those Connecticut years included regular travel in and out of New York City to take classes and begin to study seriously with Dan Wagoner, Viola Farber, and Merce Cunningham, finally leaving marriage in 1975, becoming Judith Ren-Lay (my full maiden name with a stripe added for services rendered to marriage). Katherine Gallagher, JoAnn Jansen and I, three women leaving marriages, sublet a railroad apartment on Mott Street between Spring and Prince and joined the dance company of Gus Solomons jr.

I toured with Gus for the next five years including the *California Institute of the Arts* where we became the resident company traveling back and forth between east and west coasts. The company at that time was Gus, Donald Byrd, Katherine Gallagher, Jack Apfel, Nanna Nillson, Reudi Brack, Sussana Weiss, Pat Graf and Carl Thomson. Ruis Woertendyke and Mio & Beo Morales also joined as support in lighting and music. In those days it was possible to live

17

cheaply and be a member of a company collecting unemployment during off seasons to supplement the nominal rehearsal and performance pay.

Then while on tour performing a solo Gus had made for me, I found myself spilling out of the forms and improvising something else. Gus asked afterward "what was that?" I really didn't know. It had come upon me as total possession. I just danced out of the movement I had been given. It was becoming clear to me that set choreography was not to be the end of my explorations into movement and performance.

7. NEW YORK   circa 1980   (photo Frank Siciliano)

~~~~~~~~~~~~~~~~~~~

Resolve

This is the time. I have completed all the work put before me to do. I will enjoy fulfilling this piece that has been developing. I have no idea what it is about, what it means, or even how it may be received. I only know that I have been engrossed in the process and feel strongly about some of what has been resolved. I am not completely free from fear and mind-games about my competency. I suspect some will like it, others will not. It's in the doing that I gain my life, pulling it all together and throwing it out into the world in order to complete a current cycle of changes.

~~~~~~~~~~~~~~~~~~~

Hot Cloud Mountain 1979

Since my first divorce in 1968 I had begun keeping journals, writing down songs, poems, ideas, dialog, scripts – whatever was occupying my mind. The voices began to insist themselves. I labored over the words, the language, until I was ready to trust the writing to be the core of a concert piece billed as *a dance for four women in sixteen sections / a play for three men in two acts* – performed in September 1978 for three nights at the *Lotus Gallery*, a loft in SoHo. This began my shift from dance to performance. I called it *Hot Cloud Mountain*.

The cast was Susan Hendrickson, Neal Klein, Robert Levitan, Mimi Pawlowski, William Wesbrooks and Catherine Zimmerman, with music by Pat Graf.

HOT CLOUD MOUNTAIN
Program

ACT I

Cream..Judith
It's So Hard...
   The Questioner...Robert
   The Philosopher...William
   The Biographer..Neal
Windmills...the women
Push/Pull...Mimi, Susan
Philodendron..Susan
Aria..Mimi
Brush-off..all
Fast/Slow...Susan, Catherine
Spacing..Catherine, Mimi
Swinging..all
Chasing Tails...the women
Mirror..Catherine
Follow-through...the women

ACT II

Possibilities..Judith, the men
Concentration
   What, How, Why......................................the men
   (a word score for 3 voices)
   34 Forwards and Backwards............................the women
   (movement phrase to reverse at any time, scored for three)
Circles Changing Focus.......................................the women
Sit, Stand, Lie...men & women
Falling Around...men & women
Finale..all

8. CASSANDRA'S QUILT Warren Street Performance Loft 1981 (photo Richard Bull)

9. PEARLS STRUNG ON DREAM SONGS Re-Cher Chez 1981
(photo Robert Grasmere)

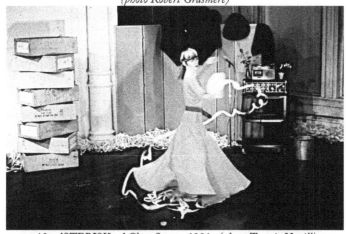

10. ASTERISK A Clear Space 1981 (photo Tannis Hugill)

21

I continued to write terse scripts with songs, perform specific tasks, actions and movement. I was living on my own at 42 Grand Street in SoHo, where I still reside, a small 3 room apartment passed to me by Suzette Theodorou, a friend from my time at the University of Maryland who moved to Vermont with her husband to start a family.

In *Cassandra's Quilt 1981* I told the Greek tale of Cassandra and Apollo (how he spit into her mouth so no one would believe her prophecies) while I sang and danced to sounds of newspapers being cut and torn up with radio and television broadcasts blaring (Billy Jean King announcing she was gay on the radio in one performance) eventually sweeping it all away with a giant broom and then setting fire to it in a bucket as the piece ended and the only light on my face was that fire.

In those early pieces I changed and changed and put on and took off and arranged and chose and changed and discarded and obtained and changed and changed and changed – clothes, while dancing and singing in a total frenzy of action.

I've eaten roses, lit yard long sparklers, spread mud on my face, walked around with rubber gloves on my feet, dismantled a paper skeleton, threatened the audience with a cleaver, sung Brownie Scout songs, bounded around on pointe shoes in my mother's wedding dress with swim googles on, attacked satin roses with giant scissors, stuffed cheese boxes, shot feathers from a bow, spun tops, wrapped myself in foil, set off firecrackers, blown up balloons, lit spaces with candlelight and flashlights, burned incense, eaten a banana, fought with an umbrella, hid behind a tumbleweed, perched on a stool, and spun with a roll of 1980's computer tape collecting at my ankles.

I created installations from whatever I could find, dismantle and utilize. Eventually I was cutting apart family heirloom quilts and hand sewing the pieces back together again to form a mandala backdrop.

~~~~~~~~~~~~~~~~~~

Origin

My first form was dance – the body as instrument, life force as material, a compositional awareness defined by a study and understanding of the complexities and interactions of space, time and energy. This grounding in an aesthetic language of the human body, gave rise to acts of being one with all materials, in a constantly active and changing process, reorganizing the elements at hand, restructuring meaning as it is found in moments of occurrence.

~~~~~~~~~~~~~~~~~~

11. WOW FESTIVAL 1981 (photo Mariette Pathy Allen)

12. ASTERISK 1981 (photo Tannis Hugill)

Songs Off the Fringe 1980-84

During this time I was also writing down remembered dreams. Recording engineer Todd Anderson, who had access to a good rate at a studio in the basement of Manhattan Plaza where he worked, recorded them along with the many vocal and percussion sounds I had begun to make. They became the *Dream Songs* and the background sound score for several performances at that time – *Continuous Work/ Current Parts, Twelve Pearls Strung On Dream Songs, Asterisk-* performed at ReCherChez and Tannis Hugill's A Clear Space.

I had learned from early experiences in New Haven how difficult it was to keep a performing company together, especially without regular paying gigs. I needed time to work out the trajectory of the work. With the exception of *Collaborations: Where The Fish-Net Hose Sunk Deep-Cut Into The Purple Navel Of My Cabbage Sandwich 1980* (performed with 3 dancers and a 3 piece rock band at the Warren

Street Performance Loft), *Categories Of Unrest 1983* (with Lucy Sexton, Anne Iobst, Jo Andres and Jean Brassard on the roof of Riverside Church), *Stake 1983* (with Gerry Hemingway doing the music live and Lucy Sexton and Anne Iobst dancing with me at PS 122), I devised ways where I could do most everything myself – often even running the lights from the stage. At this point I was turning out solo pieces with taped and live sound, performing in small clubs and performance venues culminating in *Songs Off The Fringe* at the Pyramid Club after which, at the recommendation of Lois Weaver and Peggy Shaw, for whom I had performed many times at WOW, I was invited to Europe to perform at the Melkweg in Amsterdam. People were beginning to notice the work and I had even received some positive reviews. Once in Europe I stayed for 5 months booking solo gigs wherever I could in London, West Germany and Amsterdam, opening for rock bands at clubs, staying with friends, often sick, cold, hungry, frequently lost, making publicity flyers from placemats found in restaurants and, in spite of the hardships, convinced I was doing what I needed to do.

13. MINOR VENOM 1983 (photo Dona Ann McAdams)

I returned to NYC and promptly created *Minor Venom 1984* featuring film by Merrill Aldighieri and an installation of sheets of plastic through which the film was projected. This piece was all about addiction, featured a fabric dragon, spreading rice with a shovel, ending with a medley of new songs, written during my travels.

14, 15. MINOR VENOM 1983 (photos Adam Peacock)

I was beginning to feature the recordings, still facilitated by Todd Anderson with a growing book of songs. The site specific challenges of a changing space brought time into the moment, and the development of soundscapes contrasted with live singing, began to increasingly interest me. Movement continued to be the center of the work, but not choreography. Set, learned moves no longer drew me. Improvising on the moment seemed to be the way to go forward.

16, 17, 18. CATEGORIES OF UNREST Roof Of Riverside Church 1983
(photos Dona Ann McAdams)

29

~~~~~~~~~~~~~~~~~~

Process

Focus is on connections; what brings elements together and what pulls them apart — working with many divergent forms of language, sound, objects with physical properties, movement — to reveal fresh structure in the combining process. I traverse the gaps between reality and desire, actuality and dream, possibility and fantasy, while maintaining a heightened, mindful state of deep awareness. Through relationship and context, new meanings emerge, as I give myself over to forces that inform my search for choices to illuminate the human condition in our present era of frantic fractal concerns lusting after all known forms of evil distraction. How does one persist in processing life into work, surviving creatively against all odds, to live in a constant state of process and practice? I give myself over to a growing awareness of what it is to be alive, keeping a prolific journal for 50 years as primary source material.

~~~~~~~~~~~~~~~~~

19. THE GRANDFATHER TAPES PS122 1985 (photo Dona Ann McAdams)

The Grandfather Tapes 1985

When my grandfather, Earle C. Haas (the doctor who invented Tampax in the 1930's and who was a pioneer in birth-control research) was in his 90's my sister recorded seven hours with him telling stories from his life. She passed them to me and I applied to Franklin Furnace where it was first performed in January of 1985. *The Grandfather Tapes* became a two-hour solo based on those live recordings, which became the sound score for the piece.

After touring California and Colorado, *The Grandfather Tapes* was honored with a New York Dance and Performance Award, the *Bessie,* for outstanding artistic achievement in creating "a courageously personal world of family and legacy."

The overall score was conceived in categories of universal life passages alternating between the recorded life of my grandfather and my own reflections on my life so far.

This piece, having been commissioned, led to a total obsession of detail in scoring. I edited the tapes by ear, cutting seven hours into one. Then categorized the cuts and interspersed live, spoken text including several folk songs, and a long improvised dance to the story of the invention and sale of Tampax.

The piece opened with me sitting in a rocking chair reading from a book *100 Makers of the 20th Century* in which my grandfather is cited. At one point I dressed as my grandfather and even shaved myself with his straight razor. It was performed on three platforms of varying heights and the room was filled with wood chip sawdust creating an environment that smelled of fresh cut wood.

The Grandfather Tapes **Program / Structure**
Introduction
Opening
Memory 1
Aging
Beginnings
Work Skill 1
Memory 2
Communication
Pioneering
Prejudice
Death/Fear
Violence/Sex
Father
Mother
Work Skill 2
Children/Time
Personalities
Entertainment
Music
Memory 3
Profession
Dignity/Reality
Survival Systems
Waves
Environment
Success
Pressure
Expansion/Awareness
Regret
Confirmation

20. THE GRANDFATHER TAPES   PS122 1985   (photo Dona Ann McAdams)

~~~~~~~~~~~~~~~~~~

Structure

A project begins with just the tiny seed of an idea – a thought, a fact, a word, a dream. Then gradually elements are added, constantly reconfiguring the whole. Each addition finds a place and changes the direction ever so lightly to fully realize the growing demands of new ideas as they accumulate. Structures emerge. These structures are works of art. They contain our lives Making art is a compulsion of identity and meaning, constantly shifting. Through isolating and assimilating each incident of action, the work comes as we figure out how to incorporate separate elements into a whole.

~~~~~~~~~~~~~~~~~~

21. ORPHAN 1986 (photo Nancy Curtis – Denver)

Fortunate Collaborations 1986-1990

In *Like Someone I Saw Quickly In The Moonlight Running Across The Lawn* performed in Denver in *1986* for the First Denver Performing Arts Festival I asked a group of local performers to begin on the outside of the performance space in the dark, improvising their way from the edges of the room to the center making whatever sound and movement they felt. Then we directed one spotlight into the space controlled by Mark McCoin who improvised where and how long to shine it, moving it through the space like another performer in response to what was happening. The piece ended when the light went out.

As my work developed in subsequent pieces, the aural score became more and more complex combining live and recorded sounds and miked voice. Soon I was performing with live musicians.

A vibrant punk scene dominated music with bands like Sonic Youth, Patti Smith, Hugo Largo and the Ramones. The New York city performance world of the late 80's early 90's was alive with experimentation. We enjoyed frequent opportunities in venues and clubs (*The Pyramid, The Mudd Club, 8BC, CBGB's, WOW Cafe, A Clear Space, King Tut's Wah Wah Hut, Kamikaze, PS 122, Warren*

Street Performance Loft, Franklin Furnace, LaMama, Danspace Project and Poetry Project at St. Mark's Church, Theater for the New City, Ohio Theater, The Knitting Factory, Henry Street Settlement, Westbeth Theater, Cafe Bustelo, Dixon Place, Roulette, ABC No Rio and many more).

These strange songs I was writing seemed to beg for an ensemble and soon Mio Morales, once music director with the Solomons Company/Dance joined me in creating *Soup*, a quartet with Beo Morales and Mark White. *Soup* was a critical success and performed at *Roulette, The Performing Garage, King Tut's Wah Wah Hut, ABC No Rio, Cafe Bustelo,* and *The Knitting Factory*, but keeping a group together was not my strength. We lasted most of 1988 and then I was back on my own.

22, 23. SOUP 1988 *(photos Jim Clayburgh)*

36

Called back to Denver in 1989 when my mother became ill, I met a group of musicians who embraced my work and became ongoing musical collaborators – Mark Fuller, Bob Drake, Mark McCoin, Patrick Bowers. With their inspired help I was able to expand my musical explorations, creating *Orphan*, a paean to the death of my mother. Also met life-long collaborator Jud Hart at that time, now a San Francisco artist.

24, 25. ORPHAN 1986 (photos Dona Ann McAdams)

To The Beat Of Impossible Causes 1990 was created in response to my 1989 emergency open heart surgery. Drake, Fuller and McCoin worked from a mock-up sound score and we put the piece together long distance. Each of them was a musical inspiration to me.

Mark Fuller is now a sound designer and engineer, first based in Los Angeles now relocated to the Bay area with MarkFullerMastering. Bob Drake keeps his music alive creating recordings of his own and for others at his incredible studio in Borde Basse, France, and Mark McCoin, a professor of music for many years at Colorado University, now re-located to the University of Texas at San Antonio. I consider them all artists of the highest degree. They taught me to trust myself, value my work and honor a way of working that's never about career and always about a deeply resonating evolving quality in service to humanity.

Another collaborator who taught me about quality work is Stephen Petrilli, an extraordinary lighting designer now based in Boston. From 1986 when he first saw *Orphan* and offered to work with me, subsequently designing the lights and even building a light-board for a small performance at *Dixon Place*, he has been my choice for lighting design. I asked for him whenever a lighting designer did not come with the gig. He always made things better, took on the rough situations with expertise and aplomb whether on tour or in NYC. Donald Byrd once told me in reference to Stephen's designs "his lights love you". A consummate artist he refuses to do jobs he can't relate to, letting his values rule his choices.

Through the first 2 decades, I relied on photographer Dona Ann McAdams to support and document the work. Her rare eye and great capacity for love and caring became reliably close to my creation of the work both as inspiration and great friend.

26. *PSYCHE'S CRIB LA MAMA 1988* (photo Dona Ann McAdams)

Psyche's Crib 1988

The last piece I performed before my heart exploded and I was out of commission for many months was *Psyche's Crib 1988* at *LaMama*. I created an installation of a clothesline strung with white sheets and clothes, instructing *La Mama's* resident lighting designer Howard Theiss to use it as a canvas and simply paint with his lights. Old friend Ed Harker created an electronic score and Nancy Spanier helped me by directing the ensuing monolog. After I performed a long solo dance to a Bach cello concerto, a few of my performance friends (Jo Andres, Lucy Sexton, Anne Iobst, Frank Conversano, Sanghi Wagner, Jean Brassard) made a brief appearance as they rushed up from the audience, moved set pieces in and stuck labels on me – drawings made on post-its. I had spent a number of weeks in Denver with my mother before her death and was reading about the cribs in the Old West where prostitutes worked. I had also been reading about Alchemy, most particularly in *The Psychology of the Transference* by C. J. Jung.

I also found photos of woodcuts from the *rosarium philosophorum, secunda pars alchimiae de lapide philosophico* (Frankfort 1550). Turned into slides and projected onto sheets, they depicted a process of Alchemy as it is conceived in the transference of the subconsciousness through psychotherapy.

<u>from the program:</u>

The Mercurial Fountain

King and Queen

The Naked Truth

Immersion in the Bath

The Conjunction I

The Conjunction II

Death

The Ascent of the Soul

Purification

The Return of the Soul

The New Birth

Psyche: a mythological figure who, after much travail, accomplishes four tasks set for her by Aphrodite – sorting seeds, gathering the golden fleece, filling a crystal goblet with water from the river Styx, and obtaining a cask of beauty ointment from Persepone in the underworld. When the tasks are completed, she and Eros are married and she gives birth to a girl named Pleasure.

Crib: 1) a baby's bed   2) a single operation run by a prostitute in business for herself in Colorado around 1878.

"The god of death is the lord of sex and the dance...that which dies is born. You have to have death in order to have life – loss, death, birth, loss, death – and so on."   Joseph Campbell

"...you'd better not get caught in a symbolic situation. You don't have to die really, physically. All you have to do is die spiritually and be reborn to a larger way of living."   C.J. Jung

27. PSYCHE'S CRIB LAMAMA 1988 (photo Dona Ann McAdams)

~~~~~~~~~~~~~~~~~~

Affect

Rejection of the new or unique often involves an inability to perceive something presenting an arresting dynamic – one that isn't observed in the usual run of choices, one that requests the observer to take a fresh look which might have the effect of changing thought. Beliefs driven by ambition can make one very vulnerable to error, wasted energy, and slavery to pre-existing disciplines no longer valid within currently changing reality. Take seriously comments of those who, seeing your work for the first time, with no stake in it and not knowing anything about you personally, appear to like it, tell you they like it, and seem helpful towards its continuance.

~~~~~~~~~~~~~~~~~~

28. TO THE BEAT OF IMPOSSIBLE CAUSES 1990 (photo Dona Ann McAdams)

~~~~~~~~~~~~~~~~~~

Forms

Artists begin with a vision, develop a philosophy, study and then choose a form which can most clearly contain their conceptualization of the way things can be, or are, or were. If the study of the form becomes only an exploration of the history and development of that form, then all the fresh vision which led to it is lost and the work fails as art.

I believe that art is not manipulation of craft (the artisan) or solving problems (the technician or scientist) or playing games (the gambler or athlete) – it is an act of bringing into focus some aspect of living that unites body and mind with feeling, a task of recognition and development, of communication and epiphany, of ritual and realization.

~~~~~~~~~~~~~~~~~~

29. *UNDERCURRENT EVENTS PS122 1991 (photo Dona Ann McAdams)*

Undercurrent Events 1991

Returning to performance after taking nearly a year to recover from open heart surgery, with the creation of *To The Beat Of Impossible Causes*, it was time to take a good look at the mixed media performance work I had been turning out. The critics were always generous, but I sensed I was losing my way.

Undercurrent Events came from my ongoing collaboration with Dona Ann McAdams, the resident photographer at Performance Space 122 who had become a close friend. I was interested in her photography beyond her stunning performance shots, so I spent time with her archive and conceived of a piece where we could make a selection of her photographs into slides projected onto the back wall of the performance space. The installation would be newspapers covering every inch of the space with the fine print pages serving as projection screens. Lighting was by Stephen Petrilli and the recorded sound score expertly run by Marion Appel.

At that time I had obtained a 4 track cassette recorder. During an extended residency at the University of Colorado, I created and recorded all the music to be played behind my singing voice –

sometimes percussion, sometimes tracks of voices, all inspired by 12th Century antiphons, responsories, sequences and hymns. I also used a radio mike for the first time incorporated into the black and white costume as a necklace. As inspiration for the script I used Ken Follett's novel *The Pillars of the Earth* and Sun Tsu's nine situations from *The Art of War* written in the 6th Century BC noting that 'only the gender had been changed'. This served as the structure for the piece.

> DISPERSIVE GROUND – The Shape of the Weapon
> FACILE GROUND – Leading Despot
> OPEN GROUND – Listening Shield
> INTERSECTING GROUND – Seeding Woman
> CONTENTIOUS GROUND – Breathing Child
> SERIOUS GROUND – Prowling Violence
> DIFFICULT GROUND – Raking Man
> HEMMED IN GROUND – Taunting Absurdity
> DESPERATE GROUND – Plunging Will

from the 1991 publicity:

> Ren-Lay turns her peeled eye towards illusion – personal and political. A work of fiction, like today's news, based in what might sort of be happening, but creating an illusion of seeming to be something else. Layers of chants and songs in a cacophony of voices. Layers of light hitting below the belt. Layers of paper, streams of paper, black and white. What is told and what lurks beneath the surface, exhumed, alive and rumbling. It's the Dark Ages. The weak are in power spoiling the larger picture. A 12th Century abbess sits in her monastery writing ecstatic chants while newspapers from the end of the 20th Century camouflage the value of dissent, and artists and intellectuals run for the cover of classical codes to survive a rise in military fervor and the monopoly of wealth and power by the few unenlightened, unimaginative individuals who gather the masses to their cause with slogans while covering up the proliferation of inhumane and fearful tactics. A new solo celebrating light and exhuming the spirit of hope from a burial of newsprint.

30, 31. UNDERCURRENT EVENTS 1991 (photos Dona Ann McAdams)

~~~~~~~~~~~~~~~~~~

Expansion

I have viewed life from a detailed sensitivity of possible human movement (dancer/choreographer), from a tin-eared jangle of human sounds and languages (singer/vocal composer), from a juggle of words to carry the flow of changing feelings threaded with ideas and spirit (poet/spoken text), and from objects bought & found, photographed, drawn, collected, ordered, worn, varied, utilized, stored, revisited (visual artist), all while choosing and juxtaposing available spaces and shared proximity.

~~~~~~~~~~~~~~~~~~

32, 33. FOOT/TONGUE/WEB ST. MARK'S CHURCH 1992
(photos Dona Ann McAdams)

Foot/Tongue/Web 1992

For my first piece for St. Mark's Church with the Danspace Project commissioned by Laurie Uprichard, I wrote:
"It's very odd and minimal – my last piece was talk, talk, talk – in *Foot/Tongue/Web* I don't say a word."

Creating a site-specific installation in this venerable space was the challenge and my choice of material was rolls of elastic, like the kind that holds up your underwear. When stretched between the pillars in a particular way they created a line drawing in space which met, web-like, at the apex. Carol Mullins lit the piece, brilliantly illuminating the white lines.

> **From the press release:**
> *Foot/Tongue/Web* deals with elements of hunger, seduction, freaks and broken parts evoking the interiors of cathedrals, caves, and dreams while the performer becomes animal, alien, child and crone. With choreographic contributions by Gus Solomons jr, Susana Hayman-Chaffee and Jo Andres, music by Mio Morales, projected photos by Dona Ann McAdams and lighting design by Carol Mullins.

> **From the program:**
> In some Native American languages, like the Navajo and the Quechua, the past, our history, what we know and what we can see, lies in front of us and the future is behind. So they would say we back into the future – go through life facing backwards.

I entered walking backwards with a repetitive walking pattern into and out of the visible doors. Jack Anderson called them "portals" in his NY Times review. He also wrote "her undiscovered country is life, itself."

I used the occasion to create my first chapbook of poems and drawings *Age Of Descent* given out to the audience.

34. FOOT/TONGUE/WEB   St. Mark's Church 1992
(photo Dona Ann McAdams)

~~~~~~~~~~~~~~~~~~

Presentation

It is the connection between forms and not the forms themselves that has defined my line of inquiry, having evolved through creating and showing a varied and extensive body of original works of choreography, performance art, music, poetry, interactive installation, photo collage, digital photography, drawing and small sculpture.

~~~~~~~~~~~~~~~~~

Separation of Parts 1995

As the years passed and the work accumulated I often took time to consider, to move closer to process and rediscover just what I was up to. I had begun drawing while recovering from open heart surgery and Dona offered me a solo show at the *SpaceCase* gallery she curated in the hallways of *PS 122*. I called it *Offer The Stroke/Stroke The Offer*. Fully installing two windows of approximately 40 drawings led me to focus on the various parts of my work being separate from one another. At this point I was realizing how demanding it had become to keep up all the forms I had touched into. There was now a large portfolio of drawings, hundreds of songs (some recorded, some not) more poetry than I could keep track of, an apartment full of installation and costume elements and small sculptures. More and more I was required to pull the work into pieces to become part of group shows, to appear in benefits, to adjust the work so it might be seen. The world seemed to want me to diminish what I offered, to pin it down, to reduce it into digestible bits.

Separation Of Parts was an experiment in focus, to narrow the scope and see what parts seemed to have a future, pulling elements apart to focus on each separately – visual flat work, dance, vocal music. It was an exercise in discovery to determine how best to go forward. It consisted of the *SpaceCase* show of drawings *Offer The Stroke/Stroke The Offer*, *Space Pie* and *Scale Slicing*.

Space Pie, a solo dance in silence sliced the performance area at St. Mark's Church into parts of a pie – that desired pie so few could access whole. It was all about scarcity and limited availability. It was never documented, largely because I had broken a bone in my foot prior to performance and was dancing injured, so I cancelled the videotaping. After the fact, it seems appropriate that its life was only as a live experience for those assembled and otherwise does not exist.

Early on I had railed against everybody asking for video of my work when applying for grants and gigs. I said "I don't make video work, I make live work." This purism did not feed my career. In response I made a few made-for-video pieces, but eventually succumbed to the documentarians going forward. Now, in recent pandemic years, all experiences have become virtual and distant.

Who could have known we would become a community only accessible by video or on computer-driven on-line points of contact? All purism has had to be diluted and reality has become something else entirely.

Scale Slicing, a solo vocal opera, was performed at *The Knitting Factory*, my creative home for the rest of the 90's into 2002, the year my album *Out Of Nowhere* was released on the *Knitting Factory* label. The music had begun to lead the way. Michael Dorf commissioned a sound score for his series *Loud Music/Silent Film* and I composed and performed with Ken Butler to a 1921 Swedish classic called *Witchcraft Through The Ages 1995-2001*. I had begun to extend my voice and process it to find new sounds. My vocal range had grown and, juxtaposed with Ken's hand-made instruments, this score to a projected film definitely had legs. We performed it every Halloween for many years, toured with it to Chicago, San Francisco and New Haven and even revised it, at the request of old friend Norman Frisch who was curating the arts center at *Snug Harbor*, the retired civil war sailors home on Staten Island. We performed, this time with Satoshi Takashi on percussion, in *The Old Chapel*, a spooky relic from the 1800's, on October 2001 – the first performance after watching the towers come down on 9/11.

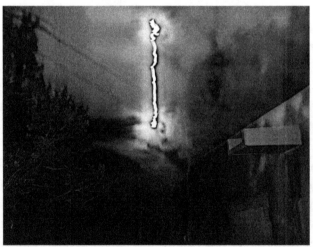

35. FALLING MOON IN CLOUDS (digital photo) j.r-l.

~~~~~~~~~~~~~~~~~

Validation Deprivation

The chaotic concept of allowing individual and conflicting truths to exist simultaneously in interaction is difficult since it has the effect of deflating ego, which we often think, erroneously, is the source of spirit, motivation and confidence. It's so easy to fall prey to the fascinating powers of manipulation which surround us all. Then there are the things we did not mean to do and have regretted afterward. We wonder, when the going gets tough, is someone somewhere saying "no" when our name comes up? Can we be so invested in being ourselves, we have little control over the affect we may have?

~~~~~~~~~~~~~~~~~

Fallow Fields 1996-2002

The years flew by. My sister joined my mother and father in death. I seemed to always be knocking with bloody knuckles on the brick wall of acceptance by the cultural powers of NYC. I kept making work, performing wherever and whenever I was invited, but my meager applications seemed to always end in rejection and I was once again forced onto my own impulses to get the work seen. Few champions to the work emerged.

Gus Solomons jr and Molissa Fenley hired me to help them bring a fresh eye to their work and I served them and a few others from 2004 to 2010 as *The Performance Doctor*, using that *unfailing touch* the director from the University of Maryland production of *Oklahoma* had, in 1970, attributed to me. It was a big change to be paid for my expertise and I was grateful to be considered an asset.

There were individuals and venues who still knew of me, valued my offerings and would invite me for the occasional small gig, but I was becoming marginalized. This caused me to further withdraw just at a time when visibility was most needed. Friends kept telling me, with my substantial body of work, I would soon be 'discovered.' Norman Frisch thought I would be a perfect thesis for the new era of doctorates given in performance art. Even into my 70's there remained hope for possible discovery and wider exposure which might invite the *rising of the cream*. But my decades of offerings had resulted in an experience of anonymity. I felt I had lost the fight to be known. I sensed the worlds of dance, performance, music, and poetry had moved on without me.

36. photo Dona Ann McAdams

~~~~~~~~~~~~~~~~~~

Compulsion

We find a way to work when we are driven to create. Even when the world seems to cast a blind eye, we must make things. Being an artist is not a choice, it is a rigorous calling.

~~~~~~~~~~~~~~~~~~

37. *JUD HART EXHIBITION* San Francisco 2004
(photo Jud Hart)

Infrequent Exceptions 1993-2010

I was in residence and performed several times at the *New Arts Program* in Kutztown, PA at the invitation of James Carroll. Every year he still invites me to submit to his *Small Works Salon* and I have had pieces of sculpture, drawing, photography and a book exhibited there.

Gus Solomons jr commissioned a sound score for a piece he was choreographing with his last company *Paradigm* featuring a venerable group of dancers over 50 including Gus, Carmen DeLavallade, Michael Blake, Valda Setterfield, Dudley Williams, and Keith Sabado. The piece, *Gray Study 1999* was my first and only time to compose music for dance. I was a bit out of my element, but the recording was facilitated by Jim Poupoulis at Amphion Music and the company performed it many times. In a 2002 performance

I added a live vocal part based on writings from 9/11, as an addition to the recorded score.

At this time I was also still working with strings of elastic whenever an installation was called for. Elastic had such strong intention. It was able to tie things together, snap them apart, receive projected light, hold things up, wrap furniture, hang other elements, tie and wind itself through and over obstacles, define a space, and serve as an ultimate symbol of flexibility, motion, and connectivity.

In *The Last Taboo* a short piece for a *PS122* benefit in 1993 I folded up long strings of it and pinned them to key parts of my jumpsuit proceeding to hand them out one at a time to audience members, tying myself to them. When I told them to 'let go' all at once the strings snapped back to me with a visual and sound dynamic that was not only surprising, but very funny.

38, 39. THE LAST TABOO 1996 (photos Dona Ann McAdams)

40. INVISIBLE EVIDENCE OF OUR ANGELIC RESIDUE 1994
(photo Dona Ann McAdams)

For *Invisible Evidence Of Our Angelic Residue 1994* at LaMama, elastic strings held up a life-size anatomically correct paper skeleton and became angel wings as the skeleton soared over the space while several guest musicians performed with me in delivering a live musical evening. Joining for this piece was Laurel Jay Carpenter who helped put the skeleton together, Matthew Kobalkin, Jalalu-Kalvert Nelson, Mio and Beo Morales, Craig Gordon, Bea Licata, Edie Ellis, Elise Kermani, Michael July and Ann Klein.

At the time I wrote: "This piece is a process of weaving together divergent lines of aural information (poetry and songs with live music) into a whole – avoiding category so the audience is never sure if they are at a poetry reading, a music concert, a formal theater piece, or an off-the-cuff happening."

In 1996 I was once again injured and laid up for some months. Seems like every time this happened I was able to create some kind of flatwork. In 1990 it was drawings, this time it was photo collage. At that time I had been having photos developed by mail, since everything had not yet gone entirely digital. Some prints came back with an abstract image where the intended shot had gone off focus.

I requested double photos, and began arranging the shots to create an abstract of the images contained in the photos. I then began shooting items and corner walls in my apartment and collaging them into rather large abstractions. *Corners Of A Room – SpaceCase Gallery 1997* became my second solo art exhibition.

Still grateful to have a creative home at *The Knitting Factory* on Leonard Street, close to home, I performed a piece I called *Boomerang 1997-1999* in 7 incarnations – *Breath Alert, Warp Spasm 1, Warp Spasm 2, Cart Before The Horse, Warp Spasm 3, The Best Laid Plans, The Pen Is Mightier Than The Pig*. Based in an extended delay of voices it was an evening long piece conceived in language and sound often obscured by processing and overlay.

41. BOOMERANG 1997 (photo by Dona Ann McAdams)

Music continued to be the focus. For *In Consistency 1996-97* I booked 5 nights at the Knitting factory for improvised duets with master musicians Allan Jaffe, Joe Gallant, Rufus Cappadocia, Ken Butler and Brett Heinz. With the help of Brett and Daniel Golderacena the sessions were recorded and, while at an off-season retreat at a health spa in upstate New York, I did an aural edit, returning to the city to create *Out Of Nowhere* – my first cd of music released by the *Knitting Factory* label in 2002.

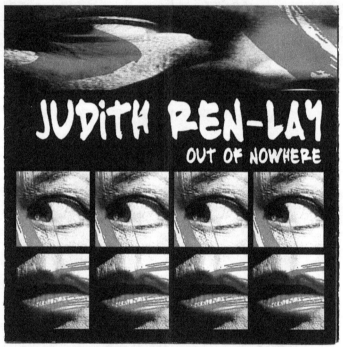

42. *OUT OF NOWHERE 2002 (CD cover design David Rodriguez)*

The year the album came out my sister, who had suffered for many years with multiple sclerosis, decided to die by assisted suicide. The time when I should have been promoting the music was spent dealing with her choice. Family insists itself upon us, even when we need to be focused elsewhere.

Out Of Nowhere was released to critical praise, but soon forgotten. I was disillusioned, but hopeful.

I later made a dance solo to several of the cuts – *Falling Eagle 2005*, commenting on American stereotypes while turning in place with a red, white and blue feather boa.

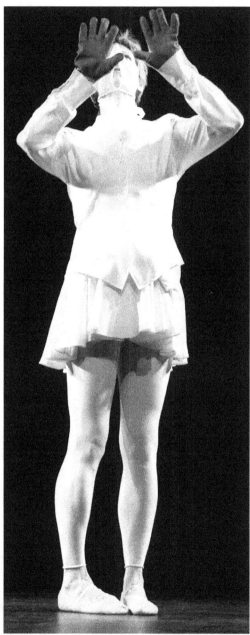

43. FALLING EAGLE 2005 (photo by Alan Lokos)

In 1999 I once again returned to Europe, this time to direct a piece by my friend Susanne Mueller in Biel, Switzerland with music by Jalalu-Kalvert Nelson. They invited me back in 2009 to perform with them at a Festival in Neuchatel and I later spent time with my old Denver friend Bob Drake at his studio/home in Borde Basse, France. We recorded some raw improvisations at that time, later featured on a cd – *Drops* – compiled in 2019 with some recordings from early work created in the 1980's.

44, 45. SWITZERLAND with Susanne Mueller and Jalalu-Kalvert Nelson 2009
(photos by Stephan Haller)

During a residency in Santa Fe, NM (facilitated by Roseanne Kadis), I had begun enjoying photography and realized my digital camera at the time (a gift from Mark Beard and Jim Manfredi) had an unusual delay between clicking the shutter and revealing the shot. Experimenting with this delay I found I could move with the camera during that gap (about 10 counts) and come up with an abstract photo of a light source. I often spent summer weeks at the beach in Ocean Grove, New Jersey with my primary focus the full moon rise over the ocean. Over several summers at Ocean Grove I practiced this process until I had a digital portfolio of dancing light figures. At the suggestion of my friend Jim Moore I showed them to Seolbin Park who curated a Digital Gallery in the east village where work was exhibited on screens and she booked a show for February coinciding with the Asian New Year – *Dances With Light – SB Digital Gallery 2010.*

46, 47. from DANCES WITH LIGHT 2010 – j.r-l.

~~~~~~~~~~~~~~~~~~~~

History

For childless artists our works become our children. Never being a mother I don't know what that experience is, but my performances became highlights of memory, special occurrences that create a road map for time spent in life. As I guide you through that map I am aware of how making work brought me purpose. Now care-taking my 'offspring' requires a need to nurture, gaining insights in how to proceed. If one's life is one's work how is that work given immortality when there is no longer a life to sustain it? I am fortunate to have been included in the music and dance collections of the New York Public Library For The Performing Arts at Lincoln Center where all traces of my work will reside for posterity.

~~~~~~~~~~~~~~~~~~~~

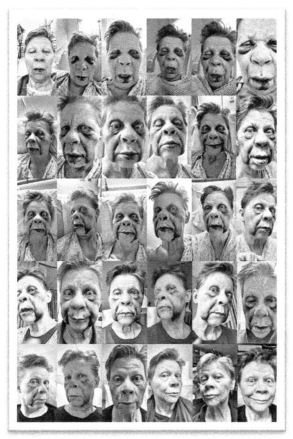

48. BROKEN FACE TRANSITIONS (digital photo collage) 2018 j.r-l.

After Disaster 2011–2021

Our lives inform our work, especially in the extremes of living. In 2011 I was hit by a cab shattering both legs requiring 5 reconstructive surgeries and several stretches of months in hospital and rehab. It was doubtful I would ever walk easily, much less dance again. Of course I wrote it out, devising a form of email communications with those who expressed concern, eventually compiling a mailing list of 300. John Jesurun told me at the time the writing was very 'direct and un-embellished.' In this way I was able to remain in communication not only with people who cared, but with the work.

In September 2018 Mindy Levokove invited me to read some of this work at the 6th Street Garden – *Canary In A Coal Mine*, later to be edited into the last book in *Quartet - Accidental Grit*.

My long delayed return to live performance happened in the fall of 2019 when Kevin Malony of *Tweed* invited me to perform at *Pangea*. I created *Crone Of Thorns* with material from my now very large portfolio of songs and writings. I was set to do the next incarnation of the growing *Crone* series – *As The Crone Flies*, in May 2020 when we were swept into a pandemic and our socially creative lives were cancelled. (*As The Crone Flies* was eventually performed at *Pangea* in September 2021).

Now 79 I have retreated into my dark walk-up cave in SoHo customized for over 40 years to serve as a refuge for this less than agile former dancer. I continue to craft words, forming the language into books.

49. CRONE OF THORNS Pangea 2019 (photo Jim R. Moore)

Considerations

I was born two years before the end of World War II. Humanity was experiencing great acts of horror and heroism. Seems like, in 2022, it still is. Change is slow and rife with indifference and ignorance, those deficit sensibilities that have motivated human beings for decades.

In the 1980's when I was first producing new performance work, I once asked my friend Robert Coe "Why am I not asked to present when so many others are?" He responded, "You have to apply."

The application process has always been my nemesis. Later I learned from Catherine Zimmerman (who was working to represent peers,) that most of her clients had available funds from trusts, family money, rich spouses, well-paying jobs or healthy grants, so they could afford to hire her and others who could handle applications and finances for them, helping to guide their careers. I did not find it inspiring to learn that career-wise, being an artist was really no different from any other profession – it's all in who you know, how much money is available, so you can afford to pay others to do aspects of the work you cannot. A staff is the most important advantage an artist can have.

All my life the world has moved faster than I can move. So much wasted time spent trying to catch up. Throughout my career I have been repeatedly required to fit into pre-existing boxes. Much of it is about how to communicate what you are doing to those who have the power to offer a larger audience or funding. The choices are too often based on 'who you know, know of, or are similar to' This has proven to be my downfall.

I never learned the lesson of how to ask for things, trusting instead to the quality of the work to carry me through. Little did I know that 'quality' was only part of the considerations in the equation of who gets seen and touted. Beyond knowing the right people, conforming to something a curator considered trendy or currently popular seemed to be required. Never really fitting in, I beat against the doors of conformity, resisted following any path other than my own, listening instead to a cacophony of inner voices.

As artists it is our job to recognize and humanize the daunting press of new truths as our reality changes. We are keepers of history, process and meaning. Those who focus only on the present are woefully short-sighted, handicapped by time and a myopic view. The long perspective of history in its excesses and errors is not available in the present. This hunger for the recent, the new – is inadequate.

As a further handicap, living through a computer or phone is like trying to navigate a life someone else seems to have control over. This is one truth we have to face. We are at the mercy of a system over which we have very limited control – searching minds locked into complex, biased systems attempting to bend the ever-changing technology to our creative will.

As I review my output of work over these now four decades, I have begun pulling from that history and find what I was writing about as early as 1980 now seems to reverberate with current circumstances. 'Before my time' is a rude reality. Pieces written many years, decades even, ago, have a resonance little of my new writing has. Time and evolution work some kind of magic. When we view classics from the past (in film, for instance) we see truth in process often missed in newer recent approaches. Classics become that for a reason. They ably capture cultural history, satisfying art's purpose to enlighten and deepen our understanding of humanity. When work is too influenced by current trends it may suffer from dilution and what Daniel Lambert once called that "damned democratization of art".

I suspect I am a bit immune to a capacity to allow chaos in. I still seek order and realize the world will never again be one of order, if indeed it ever was. The young realize this and seem capable of witnessing a myriad of variations and opinions without comparison or the futile imposition of clarity, as they seem to embrace the chaos.

When does a labor of love become a way to earn a living? Artists and non-profits rarely start out as doing anything but create ways to accomplish important things to offer the world – usually without pay. The pathways to making work pay and become self-sustaining are often few and far between, requiring a fancy tap dance towards wooing support from those who might help make a difference.

I have a suspician I never took anything I did seriously, just found ways to avoid working a regular job and to somehow, within my means and abilities, feel creative. Basically I approached my work as an escape, rather than considering it a viable contribution to culture deserving of attention or reward. I never felt I had the chops or the power to become popular, known or famous, so I never pushed for those things. Assigning myself the title of *artist* seems a self-serving conceit I probably don't deserve.

My tendency has been to bring things together in an inclusive structure to create a clear and larger trajectory. I may not have gained notoriety, but my goal in this final stretch of creative life is to offer whole glimpses into the work I have been developing and creating for many years. Whether or not it has passed the stages of 'dues paying' and 'comparisons required' does not interest me. All I can do is prepare, complete and offer. If I am not widely read at least I will have left something tangible.

Judith Ren-Lay
New York City
June 2022

50. ARRANGED TOTEM (placed sculpture) Santa Fe 2008 j.r-l.

Coda

GUARDED (song from Psyche's Crib)

51. PSYCHE'S CRIB 1988 LaMama (photo Dona Ann McAdams)

Guarded moments, guarded doors
Guarded answers, private wars
Guard the treasure, guard the main event
Guard to keep a way, from losing as we're letting go

Give all the memory of having been found free
Give a deal, give some love
Give a meal, return a welcome hug
Cause half the shadow, never goes away
So we stay in our

Guarded moments, guarded doors
Guarded answers, private wars
Guard the treasure, guard the main event
Guard to keep a way, from losing as we're letting go

Guard the secrets from the past
Guard your doubting with a laugh
Guard the heart that's beating fast
Guard the silence, guard the peace
…that's guarding you, who's guarding me?

Guard the children, guard the old
Governments would have them sold
Guard your honor, guard your death
Guard the air around your very breath
Cause half the shadow, never goes away
So we stay in our

Guarded moments, guarded doors
Guarded answers, private wars
Guard the treasure, guard the main event
Guard to keep a way, from losing as we're letting go

You can take your pleasure, take your fill
Constantly measure hidden will
But hide the matches, hold the fire
Guard against too much desire
For half the shadow, never goes away
So we stay in our

Guarded moments, guarded doors
Guarded answers, private wars
Guard the treasure, guard the main event
Guard to keep a way, from losing as we're letting go

73

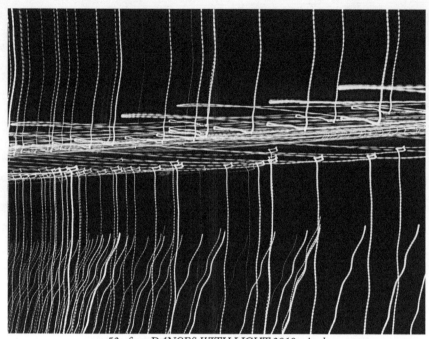

52. from DANCES WITH LIGHT 2010   j.r–l.

Facilitating and influencing individuals and organizations:

Playwrights – Eugene O'Neill, Cole Porter & Bella Spewack, George Bernard Shaw, August Strindberg, Rodgers and Hammerstein, Frederico Garcia Lorca, John Van Druten, William Shakespeare, T.S. Eliot, Samuel Beckett

New Haven Dance Ensemble – Sally Hess, Risa Jaroslow, JoAnn Jansen, Katherine Gallagher, Emmy Devine, Ceci Taylor, James Cutting, Elizabeth Kagan, Yvonne Parker, Jo Linton

New York teachers – Dan Wagoner, Viola Farber, Merce Cunningham, Nanette Charisse, Peter Saul and many others

Solomons Company/Dance – Gus Solomons jr, Donald Byrd, Katherine Gallagher, Jack Apfel, Nanna Nillson, Reudi Brack, Sussana Weiss, Pat Graf, Carl Thomson, Ruis Woertendyke, Dan Smith, Mio Morales, JoAnn Jansen

Sound Technicians – Todd Anderson, Brett Heinz, Daniel Golderacena, Beo Morales, Jim Poupoulis, Doug Westlake, Marion Appel

Lighting Design – Stephen Petrilli, Howard Theiss, Carol Mullins, Carol McDowell, Robert Wierzel

Film and Video – Merrill Aldighieri, Steve Long, Lieve Prins, Andrea Star Reese, Character Generators, Jerry De La Cruz, Charles Dennis, Jim R. Moore, Julia Heyward

Psyche's Crib **music and direction** – Ed Harker, Nancy Spanier

Soup – Mio Morales, Beo Morales, Mark White

Musician and Composer for *Stake* – Gerry Hemingway

Musician and Composer for *Foot/Tongue/Web* – Mio Morales

Denver Musician/Composers – Mark Fuller, Bob Drake, Mark McCoin, Patrick Bowers

Musicians for *Invisible Evidence of Our Angelic Residue* – Matthew Kobalkin, Jalalu-Kalvert Nelson, Mio and Beo Morales, Craig Gordon, Bea Licata, Edie Ellis, Elise Kermani, Michael July, Ann Klein

Musicians for *Witchcraft Through the Ages* – Ken Butler, Satoshi Takeishi

Musicians for *Out of Nowhere* – Ken Butler, Mark Helias, Allan Jaffe, Brett Heinz, Rufus Cappadocia, Joe Gallant

Paradigm – Gus Solomons jr, Carmen DeLavallade, Dudley Williams, Michael Blake, Valda Setterfield, Keith Sabado

Authors referenced – Ken Follett, Sun Tsu, Joseph Campbell, C. J. Jung, Sigmund Freud, Jack Anderson (NYTimes)

Photographers – Dona Ann McAdams, Robert Grasmere, Tannis Hugill, Richard Bull, Jud Hart, Frank Siciliano, Stephan Haller, Mariette Pathy Allen, Van Galligan, Alan Lokos, Nancy Curtis, Jim R. Moore, Kenneth Rinker, Suzette Theodorou, Adam Peacock, Jim Clayburgh, Tom Brazil

New York area Venues & Galleries &Curators – *SpaceCase-PS122* (Dona Ann McAdams), *New Arts Program* (James Carroll), *SB D Gallery* (Seolbin Park), *Performance Space 122* (Mark Russell), *WOW Cafe (*Lois Weaver & Peggy Shaw*) Danspace Project at St Mark's Church* (Laurie Uprichard), *The Knitting Factory* (Michael Dorf), *The Warren Street Performance Loft* (Cynthia Novack & Richard Bull), *LaMama ETC.* (Ellen Stewart, Meryl Vladamir, Nicky Paraiso), *Henry Street Settlement (*Karen Bernard*), Dixon Place* (Ellie Covan), *Clocktower* (Janene

Higgins), *The Performing Garage* (Kate Valk), *Franklin Furnace* (Martha Wilson), *A Clear Space* (Tannis Hugill), *Roulette* (James Stahley), *Snug Harbor* (Norman Frisch), *Pangea* (Kevin Malony, Steven Shanaghan, Arnoldo Caballero y Cespedes), *New York Public Library for the Performing Arts* (Cassie Mey, Linda Murray), *The Pyramid* (Brian Butterick), *The Mudd Club, 8BC, CBGB's, King Tut's Wah Wah Hut, Kamikaze, Poetry Project at St. Mark's Church, Theater for the New City, Ohio Theater, Westbeth Theater, Cafe Bustelo, ABC No Rio* and many more

Some Musical influences – Mark Dresser, Mark Helias, Ray Anderson, Allan Jaffe, Anthony Davis, Gerry Hemingway, Samm Bennet, David Simons, Mio Morales, Brett Heinz, Joe Gallant, Eliot Sharp, Sonic Youth, Patti Smith, Hugo Largo, The Ramones, Marshall Chapman, Laurie Anderson, Lou Reed, Bob Dylan, Judy Collins, Janis Joplin, Grace Jones, Fela Kute, Phillip Glass, Steve Reich, Harry Nillson, Todd Rundgren, Herb Alpert, Kingston Trio, Glenn Branca, Tom Waits, Leonard Cohen, The Beatles, The Band, David Bowie, Yoko Ono, Glen Velez, Alan Hovaness, Komitas Vartabed, John Renbourn, Sweet Honey in the Rock, Steve Reich, Sunny Ade, Los Lobos, Pauline Oliveras, Herb Alpert, Linda Ronstadt, The Roches, George Anthiell, Cindy Lauper, Tina Turner, Chanticleer, Penguin Cafe, Peter Gabriel, Flora Purim, Graham Parker, Butch Morris, Golden Palaminos, Bob Marley, Jimmy Cliff, Colin Walcott, Don Cherry, Nana Vasconcelos, Milton Nascimento, Blood Sweat and Tears, Talking Heads, Jeremy and the Satyrs, Horace Silver, McCoy Tyner, Skinny Puppy, Berlin, Santana, Lucas Foss, James Galway, The Chieftains, Walter Carlos, James Taylor, King Sunny Ade, Jaco Pastorius, Black Uhuru, Utopia, Fishbone, Hildegard Von Bingen, Native American drum and voice, Shakuhachi Japanese Flute, Pakistani Sufi music, Gregorian Chant, Tibetan Chant, Tuvan Throat Singing, Irish Dowling, Bird Songs, Hump-backed Whales, and all musicians with whom I have been lucky enough to record and perform.

53. photo by Suzette Theodorou circa 1970's

Through A Wry Kaleidoscope

a collage of edited journals

CONTENTS

54. FACES (digital photo collage) j.r–l.

Prologue - WRITING THE LIFE

Since 1968, an ongoing Journal has been my way to understand sanity, vanity, woes, triumphs, thoughts, politics, feelings about people, feelings about myself, treatises on art and dance, gleanings, soundings, planning, chronicle, diary, criticism, mysticism, readings, awarenesses, observations, communications; a moment by moment heart and soul record of living through five decades of discovery.

During this lifetime I have experienced a gnawing curiosity about how individuals get in their own way. We often obstruct our ability to realize dreams or goals, subvert our lives by remaining constantly on the defensive, always taking a battle stance to what we find along the way, often blaming others. Sometimes this is simply a matter of failing to live in the moment, but can be caused by a deep hurt, an unsatisfied need to be loved at crucial times in life. The personality is partly formed in reaction to what is presented to us as children. Each individual reacts to similar conditions differently. The more sensitive the person, the more easily they are damaged by those who do not see them, those in whose care they find themselves, those who get close and then shut down or harshly reject them. This human dilemma is a constant theme in all fiction, and everyone I know has their own story about how they got to now.

Early marriage at 19 to a closet homosexual and practicing alcoholic wrenched me from a family that loved me but was unable to offer guidance. Divorce at 23, sexually repressed in a 1960's world of open sexuality, remarriage to a man who claimed to be a cross-dresser, but was at heart a transsexual who later transitioned from male to female, all set me up for challenges accompanying intimate human relationships going forward. After two sexless marriages I eventually discovered sex and orgasm, but, in spite of trying, never have found a love I could rely on, a partner to trust, an enduring shared lifestyle with another human being.

As a substitute I cracked myself open and made art. I wrote poetry, scripts and songs; I designed environments, projected slides, danced, sang, spoke, created soundscapes and various kinds of music, eventually delved into photography, collages, drawings, small sculpture. All the while keeping copious journals in an attempt to work out through words, in language, why I was here, why I fought with life rather than living it.

At the age of 46 my body was challenged with emergency open heart surgery following a mini-stroke revealing a congenitally defective aortic valve. Then at 52 I nearly lost my right leg from a compartment syndrome caused by anti-coagulants and spent two years learning to walk again. Finally at the age of 68, approaching my 8th decade, I was hit by a speeding cab that shattered both legs landing me in hospital for six months, requiring five reconstructive surgeries and four years literally homebound. I crawled back each time, but only with the help of many people and a deep determination.

And still I am curious about life and how we get through difficulties and woundings to doggedly continue to seek some sort of meaning and purpose. Without family or devoted friends who live close, our purpose is never obvious. Living for your children or your partner offers clear motivation, often answers gnawing doubt, but living alone in a challenged, aging body, knowing that your art is all you have ever created, is daunting. I sleep whenever I can for as long as I can and let less and less of the world into my fortunate sanctuary.

Having long since dismissed religion as an answer, I refuse to be imposed upon by group adaptation to a pre-established belief system. My changing belief system is a mythology of independent choice. Even more than received heritage from family, art is our enduring link through human history, passing on an evolving human experience to those who come after us. To know what has preceded is essential to knowing how to proceed. The archeology of human history is found not only in the bones of the long dead, but in the artifacts they leave behind. If more of us don't pay attention and speak our own truth about what we see and feel now, this species may well go the way of the dinosaurs. It may anyway, but at least open voices might serve as a cry in the wilderness.

This faceted accessing of journal material necessarily touches on stories from my life, but is not intended as an autobiography. There are stories yet to tell and much writing still to do.

A haiku : on the future of curiosity

touch all you know well
search for what still needs finding
calmly keep at it

Judith Ren-Lay
New York City
June 2022

55. *photo Kenneth Rinker*

I. OFFERING

The pendulum swings between the deeply personal
and the universally applicable.
We take what is useful –
allow to pass those things with which we fail to relate.
It's a sorting process –
finding the edible bits among the roots, leaves,
stems and pods needed to grow them.

Blessing Our Choices

Hidden among the facts of our lives is more than a story, it is a compendium of choices. Darwinianly speaking, life is all about learning how to make good choices. Choice is it, even when taken to complex and multitudinous levels via art, politics, parenting, friendships, whom to mate, etc. All activities of human endeavor, as we play out this bizarre experiment, require an exercise of choice in order to live. Learning how to make our choices serve and validate our being is a lifelong challenge.

56. *FEATHER EYES (4x6 ink on paper) j.r-l.*

II. SQUEAKING THROUGH

Thoughts As Snapshots

1. *GLEANING*

A man who traveled a great distance in order to meet Emily Dickinson came away saying he was rather glad he didn't live close by, because "being with her was one of the most draining experiences he had ever had."

* * *

Native American tale about a grandfather telling his grandson that there were two wolves fighting in his heart. One an angry, vengeful one, and one a forgiving, hopeful one. "Which one wins", asks the boy. The grandfather answers "the one I feed."

* * *

Quote from the I Ching: "The heart thinks constantly. This cannot be changed, but the movements of the heart – that is a person's thoughts – should restrict themselves to the immediate situation. All thinking that goes beyond that only makes the heart sore."

* * *

A close friend suggests I have health problems because I am a great artist and have never been recognized for it. I suspect one isn't really a great artist until more than one's closest friends think so.

* * *

The accountant that lives in my head says: "stay home so you don't spend money on anything!" Her room-mate, the maintenance worker, says: "clean house, do the laundry, organize the studio, exercise daily and eat in." The traveler seems to be asleep, and the nature lover is tied up and gagged in the corner. Next week they may negotiate for a more liberal approach.

* * *

"Tradition has placed 10,000 men to guard the pass to every road in every new direction to the future." (Unknown Source)

* * *

2. *PAYING ATTENTION*

It was a summer of further body break-down, and the search for the better fitting bra.

* * *

I can be brought down by the subtlest of feather touches.

* * *

Isolation now the central unifying theme of the days as I mostly write, reaching out through my fingertips, as though little mouths were talking, letter by letter, to those I do not see.

* * *

It's always good to use my skills (which just bubble out like a mud pot in Yellowstone) once I can see the work to be done.

* * *

However do we protect and defend fragility in a driven world?

* * *

Artists, as they carve out a career path, often discover that they have created a career "trench."

* * *

It always all comes down to money, doesn't it? That is the American way.

* * *

I feel like somebody's prize toy who periodically loses an eye or a leg or some stuffing, and gets discarded for a long time because of shortcomings, only to be rescued by someone new who might enact repairs and love it again.

* * *

How stealthily the darkness seeps in and winter breeds it like dampness to mold.

* * *

3. RESISTANCE

There is a fur ball in my mind I want to cough up, get past, in order to move on with the process of breathing into the moments and finding grains of meaning as they pass.

* * *

Years after 9/11 and I'm still watching the patterns of politics – war and peace, behavior and response, stress, hopelessness, poverty and violence – as nothing seems to cut through this colorful drama of deceit and error, ignorance and arrogance. Leaders of the world seem to have no clue about how to solve the problems of our times.

* * *

Conceits of who we think we are and who we fear we are not haunt me.

* * *

I suffer from having role models who killed themselves. Since leaving two marriages, I have avoided being pulled into any 'joining' that feels unfulfilling or challenges my integrity.

* * *

We often lie to ourselves when we feel our survival (in the way we have become accustomed) is threatened.

* * *

Memory of fear, not fear itself, is what can bring us down. We can respond to fear with bravery and only afterwards are hit with the damage it can do.

* * *

Aware of the need for loyalty to source and considering other souls as equals.

* * *

I feel like a witness to my life, but not necessarily like the one who is living it.

* * *

4. CONUNDRUMS OF RELEASE

Have managed to return to an appreciation of silence.

* * *

It is *time* that concerns me now. I must become ever more efficient in its use.

* * *

I begin to see cracks in the fabric of my world and little ideas of inspiration leak in to saturate thinking.

* * *

Even my dreams have become boringly transparent. I wake up already knowing what they mean.

* * *

Isn't there a way we can practice certain modes of attachment and meaningful action without looking at it as frighteningly permanent or permanently frightening?

* * *

Life seems very strange and impossible while, when considered moment to moment, it can also seem clearly maintained and full of people and hope.

* * *

Patterning upon those we admire, takes us away from acting through essence.

* * *

Shifts of awareness happen all at once, moving us to the next plane of existence.

* * *

On reflection, I realize my demons wear the guise of lacking reward.

* * *

Cutting back on belongings is based on clearly structuring a life to cut to.

* * *

My desire to eliminate choices is in conflict with my desire to access endless ones.

* * *

It is the connections in life that make all the difference – association without entanglement.

* * *

I always come the most alive when I am preparing to "go somewhere else."

* * *

Some sort of blue taking me over. Must wear red.

* * *

All any of us wants is to believe we were actually here and our lives made a difference. Beyond that, rewards are rather meaningless.

* * *

I exist in the world as an illusion of a self I perhaps might have been. I need to close this gap and fully materialize this illusion as a self I truly am. In order to do this, I have to strongly choose a certain path and let go of all the others.

* * *

On Sundays I really miss talking to my sister, however stressful that relationship was for me. Her passing was a release, but also a great loss.

* * *

5. SAGE & PITHY

The answers are always simple, but finding them takes time.

* * *

Our objective is to not bemoan choices, but honor choices – while letting go of those one might come to regret.

* * *

Remember, it's no longer just about the work, it's also about the ability to withstand the culture and the people who are trying, however ineptly, to care-take it.

* * *

Tasks are accomplished, not only by the act of doing, but by the impulse and focus to do. We accomplish very little when we feel under physical attack from poor health, or are otherwise processing some sort of deep loss and disappointment. One has to be healthy to work in the world, as the body largely determines our quality of life. Losing physical power through illness and age, makes one more dependent and somewhat less capable.

* * *

When we move into the light, we open up darkness behind us.

* * *

There are often imperceptibly fine lines between discipline and rigidity, resolve and process, improvisation and confusion.

* * *

The way forward requires being in this world, but not of this world, participating without losing your identity, finding a navigational focus that allows for what comes, nudging you to open towards whatever might serve to assist the effort.

* * *

57. GROUND *(digital photo collage)* *j.r-l.*

III. HORSE SENSE

care of vessel is care of soul

1. *LEARNING CURVE*

Several times in this life, physical crisis struck me down and I found myself climbing out of a deep dark hole; all the focus turned to healing and a struggle to emerge from pain and limiting symptoms.

In 1989 I was diagnosed with aortic stenosis of the heart brought on by a bi-cuspal birth defect. I underwent emergency open heart surgery, got a staph infection on the table, lived in Bellevue Hospital for nearly 5 months while they tried in vain to save the valve, had a second open heart surgery and finally came home to a reality of subsistence and dependence, crawling back from near complete infirmity, on anti-coagulants for life.

In 1995 I suffered a compartment syndrome in my right lower leg, an internal bleed from the anti-coagulant, requiring 3 weeks in the hospital after a critical surgery (fasciotomy) when they thought I might lose the leg or never walk again. It was during this time I discovered the value of physical therapy. My injury was expertly treated at the Harkness Center for Dance Injuries, a revered institution started by Marijeanne Liederbach. With the hands on brilliance of Faye Dilgen, Marshall Hagins, and Marc Hunter-Hall, I learned the essential lesson that if you do a little of just the right moves every day, amazing changes can occur. After a year and a half of intense physical therapy I once again emerged whole and viable.

Then in 2011 I was hit by a cab fracturing both legs requiring seven reconstructive surgeries, eventual disability, and many years largely homebound.

Dealing with physical problems makes it very difficult to engage an ongoing, productive life. One falls short while attempting to move forward on projects or activities, and it is difficult to remain open to future possibilities. The demands of the body sit on us, insist on our attention, requiring adequate healing care and deep nurturing, no matter what the illness or injury.

Self-help is not selfish, but basic and essential. A comprehensive healthy lifestyle requires attention to detail – shopping, preparing and eating food, regular exercise periods, rest and sleep time, keeping up order and cleanliness. When we abuse our body and environment, take it for granted, treat it as though it is still what it

95

had once been, act out of habit instead of a discovery of care, we increase suffering.

It is largely attitude that makes the difference. Maintaining a balanced frame of mind is an added struggle. Our body is really quite a science project – a magical creative structure whose power and needs vary and transform significantly every decade. It is our harbinger of change.

2. *OUR BEST FRIEND*

Only in nurturing the vessel can the soul evolve. We owe it to ourselves to engage in communication with our own body. The welfare of this body, our closest physical manifestation of life is one of the most important relationships we can cultivate. Sometimes it takes ill health or pain or injury for its voice to insist on better care, but, once we begin to listen and learn how to communicate with this vessel within which life is lived and to keep it in the best possible working order, everything gets better. We rely too much on doctors and too little on actual circumstances. How do we feel when we take certain drugs or supplements? What is our energy level when eating particular foods? Is our appetite a result of emotional pain or of the body craving fuel? Do we eat because we are hungry or because we can't satisfy the cravings of years of dietary neglect? Do we drive our systems to over-achieve, putting undo stress on the skeleton, the muscles, the brain, the heart? Do we ignore the elegant machine with which we were born and allow it to fall into disuse and disease, blaming it for the natural effects of aging?

I suggest this relationship is the most important one in our lives. When we deny the wholeness that comes with thinking and feeling within the body, fail to develop a conversation of transformational change, we shorten our lives, invite in further illness and are no longer of much use to those we love. Falling back on excuses is like the airline passenger who refuses to put on their own oxygen mask in order to help others. Neglect of the body is another form of slow suicide.

So many people live in spite of their body, rather than in concert with it. One of the reasons we admire performing artists is that they lead with their bodies and often present a model of integration to the world. Physical presentation is not a superficial value, but a validation of a certain level of holistic reverence that comes about when we honor and nurture our body.

Sanjay Gupta, in his book *Keep Sharp, Building a Better Brain at Any Age*, touches on aspects of how the brain affects our lives. "The brain has one purpose – to serve the individual", he writes. He also points out the brain wants to experience joy, not live with constant toxic thoughts. Going outside our comfort zone guides the brain to strengthen its processes. Both the brain and sleep are essential to body health. I often say "go to sleep, sleep saves us." Remembering well and forgetting well are accomplished during sleep, a kind of rinse cycle bathing the brain, removing waste.

Indulge in a deep conversation with your body, listen to what it wants and don't attempt to bully it into submission as you experience changes and loss through aging and other challenges.

3. *RITUALIZING THE DAYS*

My days are conceived in organized rituals. Like saying a rosary, I count the beads as I occupy time, practicing accumulated years of yoga and physical therapy methods, most having melded into modules that can each be done in a short period of time and revisited regularly. Both aging and recovery from injury create an extreme challenge to body maintenance. Addressing this, I have created segments of focus, a product of decades of research and study. I apply what seems to work, revisit it when the area it addresses develops pain, and try to include a practice of all of them over time, some regularly, others infrequently.

I advocate a form of 'personal customization'. Take everything you know about your body in the way it responds to movement and create a program for yourself that keeps all this in mind, while adapting to changes in capacity and strength. Everybody needs a physical culture of some sort whether it be sports, gym work-outs, or personal discipline. We have to keep and refine what works for us and eliminate anything that hurts. Most important is to keep doing what feels good over the long run and that is usually what you have practiced and what you actually will do. I am not suggesting specifically what to do, but encouraging you to engage your own process and customize it through practice.

Physical therapy is essential after injury, but it is necessarily designed to be generic and must be adapted to the individual. I opt for about an hour daily 'conversation with my body' applying various techniques drawn from yoga, my own ideas from years of dance and excellent physical therapy as the baseline. Then add walking outside, when possible, or using my standing bicycle 10 minutes a day.

In a way I think of my body parts as my children, each part requiring special attention, all letting me know, through pain, what technique to apply and when. It has been many years of trial and error to discover what works. My slogan for pain management has become "if it hurts, move it, if it hurts to move it, ice it". I seem to progress under the assumption that something I am doing or not doing is causing my pain – and if I just figure out what that is, I have the power to relieve it myself.

Nearly every day, before getting out of bed, I spend 45 minutes to an hour executing a program of exercises based on physical therapy and yoga. It is designed to move all the joints – a deep conversation with the entire body in order to ascertain what state it is in before rising. Nothing is forced, but a thorough work-out first thing manages to keep pain at bay. Sometimes, when I can't sleep, I do the exercises instead of tossing and turning and, upon completion, am always able to go back to sleep. Deep rest directly after exercise is beneficial.

A partial list of my regular rituals includes: bed or mat series, standing cycle, breathing, meditation & rest, face series, weights & therabands, neck/head series, hands, voice, neti pot, supplements & eye wash. Interspersed throughout the day, most of these rituals take a few minutes at most and can be done while waiting for water to boil for tea or for an appointment or phone call. I have heard this called exercise 'snacking' – doing a targeted bit frequently for short periods of time.

A note on Yoga. Thanks to Gus Solomons jr I was fortunate to study for some years with Debby Green who taught Iyengar and from whom I learned valuable keys to practice. Yoga is many things, but for me it is a way to experience a deeply internal alignment, using leverage and stillness to challenge the body into discovering a new orientation.

Most useful for me in Yoga: four seated forward bends, tadasana/uttanasana, up and down dog, virasana, savansana, bada konasana, triknasana, warrior I & II, and both pranayama and alternative nostril breathing.

Next is to fully customize the diet. Cutting out alcohol and baked goods is the toughest, but once chosen I can manage to do it. I often operate on a yearly cycle of allowing a drink or two daily beginning at Halloween (the anniversary of my sister's suicide) through Thanksgiving, Christmas, New Year's, and my January 15th birthday. Then it is a struggle during ensuing late winter months until around April or May when I can manage to stop the alcohol and sugar completely for the next several months – through Summer and early Fall when I always feel the healthiest. Each year it is a choice whether to keep to restriction or to ease the rules and enjoy a drink and indulge in sweets and baked goods.

Life asks us to walk fine lines between work and relaxation, discipline and indulgence.

4. WALKING CHALLENGE

I call it 'mindful walking' since I am only mobile if I manifest a constant awareness of all the integrated parts of my body as I move, the careful placing of each foot, testing the terrain and adjusting to hazards. I used to just walk and let my mind operate on automatic. It was a useful creative technique, to take long walks everywhere and allow my mind to work on whatever popped in. Now I can only take 'mindful' walks where I am fully engaged – focusing directly on the activity at hand. When I danced, my body was a rich vehicle for sending the mind into the audience in hopes for a connection of thought and feeling. I can no longer experience the luxury of movement being automatic enough to free the mind. This is partly how my world has changed. without a viable left ankle. My mind must be fully engaged in accomplishing the task of walking.

I carry a walking stick, another point of essential grounding when balance is being constantly tested. Uneven sidewalk and street surfaces are like landmines and must be navigated gingerly, with focus and care, being sensitive even to the slope of the sidewalk.

When crossing a street look to see if the cross street traffic can turn into you. Preferably only cross when the cross street goes away from you if there is a choice. If not, guard your crossing by continually looking to the potential hazard. Be vocal with pedestrians who come toward you obliviously looking down, most often at their phone. A shout of "heads up" or "excuse me, walkin' here" or simply "move" can be effective. Be incensed when cars stop in the crosswalk requiring you to veer out into traffic to cross a street. Yelling and cane waving is not totally inappropriate. Focus on each foot having a secure hold on the next step, a step at a time, and be wary of all hazards, vehicular, pedestrian, surface and material. Know where you are going and keep checking up ahead in case unexpected hazards arise. Go slow with no sudden changes of direction or veering.

Every couple of blocks I find it necessary to rest/stretch. Taking time to sit and do this regularly and completely while out walking, I can resume truly refreshed, ready to carry on.

5. CONSIDERING THE PROCESS

Such a great affect weather has on the body. It is much tougher when the temperature is cold to maintain a pain-free status. Seasonal changes always dictate what's possible. However, no matter what the season, slow is the way to go when trying to do anything. Fast, sudden, unconscious actions become their own hazard. This is where massive patience is required. Accept what is, be grateful for what comes and practice patience as circumstances change.

As we grow older the burden of loss we carry is overwhelming and our view of the world is increasingly dire and fragile. We navigate layers of living, from deep to superficial. I live moment by moment with a warped sense of now and little sense of future, in an attempt to fully engage as each segment of time passes.

Remember – *gravity* is our friend. We learn to give in to it when we can and resist it when necessary, playing through the alternating dance in our own way, as long as focus is clear and a trusted process is in place for whatever is next.

58. *HUH!?* (*digital photo collage*)   j.r-l.

IV. CHASING SHADOWS

*sanity, insanity
and all the places in between*

1. DESIRES

*We all want worldly rewards
and attractive, interesting people to like us.*

Addiction

Self-doubts about who I am in the world have often flooded my senses so I engaged in a struggle to escape the condemnation of my mind, falling into mundane, vulgar rituals that appear to drive me and sustain me and energize me. But inevitably I overdo them. The rituals become more important than the affect, and a point is reached where I grow dependent on the ritual, in spite of diminishing benefit from the substance, wearing down my ability to respond freely, to see the truth of the moment.

This is the addictive mind – living under such stress and with so much fear that every choice is painfully loaded. I have learned to find healthier ways to relax and let go, allowing myself to build on habits that serve to further inform the life rather than those that say "it's ok to shut off the painful present and languish".

Easily accessible drugs, like marijuana and alcohol slow down time to the extent that one feels as though anything is possible, encouraging relaxation, taking pressure off. They also fracture thought processes so one can float on the changing moments without imposing boundaries. I suspect long-range use gives rise to an over-indulgence of the moment, believing oneself to be invincible at the expense of a firm and structured forward thinking plan cleanly related to one's core being and available gifts.

An infrequent escape into the joy and release of time slowing down, senses feeling keener, philosophical meanderings seeming to spring to mind in delicious 'eureka' moments can be useful. It is ritual, allowing release, but only truly beneficial when it disappears for extended periods of time, during which focus can be consistently sustained in order to manage the balance and awareness required to grease the wheels of a confident, responsive reality that feeds the future.

Many addictive choices begin with a need for pain control, both physical and emotional. It is the nature of problems with substance abuse that we choose it when we are experiencing pain we cannot bear. It's as though every door one might attempt to open is a potential electric shock or worse.

The prospect of pain seems to follow us everywhere, but to self-medicate, to numb the unbearable, merely prolongs and eventually intensifies one's experience of pain. The addict often exhibits a high sensibility to all forms of pain and that leads to a choice to self-medicate, bringing the comforting veil of illusion, as one is starved for rewards that come effort-free. Restorative efforts to lessen pain require a certain amount of bearable pain and inconvenience just to endure.

Heredity and Loss

Most challenging is loss of health, our own and that of those closest to us. To care for ourselves and others who may need our help, especially in a crisis situation, takes great strength and bravery.

Recently reviewed a video compilation of early family films my sister Lyn made from the old home movies. I experienced deep sadness, regret, and a little disappointment in myself that I didn't have a better appreciation of what family was. I kept landing on the solitary, changing road, trying to create something new that has power and the strength to endure a future. I see in those family movies laughter and loving through the camera, and a sense that family was the only thing that existed. The great limit in legacy was that my sister and I were never taught to ask questions, pay attention, focus, strengthen skills (other than those that earned money) or otherwise explore and create a life involved in the rest of the world outside family. I had to learn this all on my own with the occasional help of a couple of highly intelligent husbands and a myriad of driven friends. I deeply value those few who stuck with me and still inspire, nourish and encourage me after many years.

I suspect I have never fully recovered from my sister's assisted suicide. As complicated as our relationship was, at least I knew she was there for me once our parents had passed, even though we often struggled to find a way to meet on equal footing. She once told me "you are part of me" which is all very well in a romantic film, but a bit creepy when it comes to identity and differentiation of the individual seeking validation from a sibling. She battled multiple sclerosis and I suffer from a lurking guilt that I didn't dedicate my life to taking care of her.

Deaths of loved ones and close friends always take a toll. The older we get the more loss we accumulate. Grieving is a varied and personal process, but in time, balance finds us even when brought low by sad circumstances.

There is always loss. It is life's partner with gain.

2. SYMPTOMS OBSERVED

Fear is the primary cause of dysfunction
and the basis for our current reality.

Fear

We respond to fear in many ways: we leave, submit, attack, arm, or freeze. Fear is a consuming emotion; it festers, eats us up from deep inside until we recognize and release it. Since fear often leads to anger and anger is a directional emotion, when we are angry, we look for something or someone to direct it towards – if unable to do that, as with abused children, we direct it inwardly at ourselves.

Irrational Inadequacies

Sleeping long hours, reluctant to do the solitary actions necessary to continue, I swim in a lake of ennui, losing energy daily. So much information coming in. Actions of others inundate my daily reality. Still chipping away at the stone that holds firm in its position that only work validated by some outside-of-self entity is worthy. I question the value of simply making the work and resist the fight for a wider embrace of what is created.

Living in this world, with an intense need to be gratified, accompanied by growing disappointment when rewards never seem to come, is difficult. Performers, especially, exist in a vortex of need, often giving rise to demons, threatening function. It seems as though some unknown *deciders* have taken over to determine what gets made. This Sisyphean life becomes a test.

No longer, as there was when I first came to New York, is there a tiger inside, taking up the challenges, valuing the potential more than the realized, able to ignore the contrasting accomplishments of others, blinded by my own ambitions and need for recognition. Now I remain largely alone, offer what I have to give, believing deeply in the value of that, and then hear frightened voices from the darkness of silence.

My response has been to work quietly in my own way with little need to interact, cultivating anonymity. But inside I feel like a big fake thing, after over 40 years of constant output. Overwhelmed by health challenges and other inadequacies, I face an inability to function easily in what seems like a forever new and alien world. There is much confusion. My drive to create and release work is mercurial; necessary motivation ebbs and flows.

Even before the pandemic, keeping everything inside alive and ongoing, while also trying to be part of the world, was a constant challenge. I managed for years to close off from outside stimulation, but 9/11 changed all that. Now I can't seem to do things 'for the world' and also keep my own inner landscapes pruned. The outside/inside dilemma perpetuates, exacerbated by the new Covid need to distance in order to save our lives.

Nearly everybody I know appears to have figured out something to be a part of and in turn receive some sense of recompense or valuation. As time has lost relevance, I grow nervous about handling the new, experience mixed feelings about what is important to do, and shut down, desiring sugar and movies.

Comparisons Are Failed Thoughts

What is it about when we feel diminished by perceived advantages of others?

We witness lifestyles that are not our own, and then return to what is ours and find it pales in comparison. We know our own choices have led us to where we are. We perhaps regret some of those choices, as we struggle to find our way, our future, our meaning in the face of witnessing how others seem to have managed their lives. Realizing we have committed to certain irreversible decisions when there was means or advantage, as things change and possibilities diminish, a future seems to lead nowhere, hopelessness reasserts itself, and we return to a way of life that denies, resists, and persists in living without a clue about how to survive and evolve, while maintaining a balance of health.

We rue the truth that we are not someone else, someone we admire, and, instead of learning from them, we reject ourselves until, being adaptors, we lean towards a semblance of comfort, adjusting to what daily reality serves up and settling, out of necessity and limitation, for what it is we have, rather than continuing to try to get closer and closer to our imagined hope for a reality we might prefer.

Why do we believe knowing famous people will elevate our status in the world? Why is celebrity such a powerful draw? This near worship of those who have achieved what we have not, what we may desire for ourselves – is a false flag. It is diversionary at best and harmful to our own lives at worst.

Shifting Moments of Despair

I seem to have no place to put my dark side anymore. Dark talons of giving up grip me. I no longer have the spirit and fortitude to go forward with the ability to live within my means, continuing to believe things will change. Full clarity of mind, body, spirit and soul deserts me as I go bumping along day to day.

All ideas seem to melt into lost momentum and an inability to find courage and support from a larger world.

I see the fabric of what passes for reality and it appears completely transparent. I can't take it seriously. Neither can I entirely escape the fact that it's that same reality I inhabit. When we spend our lives trying to do what the world seems to require from us in order to 'succeed' we eventually realize it has all been a sham and what we appear to have wanted is no longer at all desirable.

Looking around for the next choice to make and I find myself experiencing a sinking kind of physical resignation that reads as 'do nothing'.

So I hide in my walk-up cave where a pair of blue jays are building a nest on the balcony across from my bathroom window. They stop by the fire escape periodically gathering materials. I have put out some cotton and string, but I don't know if they have found it useful. They seem to have eaten the pumpkin seeds and most of the sunflower seeds. I can hardly believe they have found me in this dark, hidden recess behind all the buildings.

3. ACTION

We are a bundle of contradictions.

Money

Like a good girl scout I am superficially prepared for disaster in terms of escape bags and supplies. But in the modern world only money is strong enough to withstand a prolonged and advanced attack. Money has become the most powerful weapon humans have created. Only nature can overpower it – as it increasingly does and will continue to do until the world realigns.

Whether you have money or not, the entire social system centers around having it – to be able to afford the housing, personal upkeep, clothes, entertainment, education, tools, gadgets, food, travel that become the center of social discourse. Most events require some sort of admission fee and people often wish to go somewhere to eat or drink which always costs money. Social discourse in the city seems to gather around some sort of café or bar or restaurant or celebration party or performance event – meeting *out*, witnessing together. Hidden in these choices is also the appearance of some level of affluence and expression of survival. In order to be part of any group, one always has to be able to pay certain dues.

Our desperate need for money is everywhere. Not only for individuals to maintain a certain quality of life, but for charities with worthy causes, government projects and candidates, to support environmental world efforts, disaster relief, ongoing assistance towards drug addiction, child and animal abuse, human exploitation and hunger all over the world. There is more need than we seem able to satisfy.

Since a 1989 health crisis, I have structured a lifestyle of subsistence, relying on the occasional contribution from friends and social security to keep my health insurance and food stamps coming.

With the golden handcuffs of a rent stabilized apartment in NYC and the benefits of being a senior citizen, I manage to keep monthly bills paid, food in, and irregular contact with a few close friends. It's a bit strange to be aware that I really live a lifestyle well below the poverty line while, at the same time, living a life very rich in necessities and things that matter. From the large perspective of the world, I am truly one of the fortunate.

Change

Having spent the years after 9/11 widening my awareness about the power structure of the world (specifically the politics of this country) I begin to see things from the prism of 'the big picture'. I am much more aware of the chronic lying that humans do to preserve their attachment to material reality and support their illusion of power in the world.

Ever since that fateful September day, when Dona woke me and I realized I had slept through the initial trauma of terrorism just blocks away, holding her hand as we watched the second tower fall from West Broadway and then staggering throughout the subsequent weeks wearing an enormous pair of rubber ears, trying to listen, trying to pay attention to what is going on in the larger world, trying to tune into news and talk radio to hear what those who are in some lane of power are saying about our condition as a country, a world, a species. I have listened for years now and it all continues to sound the same. Politics gone wrong, wars raging, criminal acts and catastrophes, natural phenomena breaking down, erupting, disrupting countless lives, loss and gain, hope and survival, pitiful examples of how stupid so many of us are, inspirational examples of how brilliant are the few.

I'm tired of listening. I am ready once again to listen to my own heart, my own mind, my inner being. I want to retreat to an inner landscape, a compendium of past experience and words of expression. I want to be selfish with my company, and never go anywhere because it may be expected as an obligation to some concept which no longer holds sway over me. Since part of socialization is to engage the lives of others, even as we focus on our own, can we be forever in the lead, even while listening?

I want to relish in the silence and allow my mind to process all that is there and value the process. Immersed in moments of grace and peace, I have become someone else. The girl/dancer/woman who came to New York in 1975 has been absorbed, erased, incorporated into some sort of accepting, coping, living, informed mechanism that begins to understand life. I am daily amazed at the capacity to do little except perform small mundane tasks, focus on time passing, being at the service of only what I seem capable of doing, while keeping up certain conversations that feed and nourish.

Choice

Choices on the moment need to be based on some sense of dreaming about the future in order to have any real strength. Most of my life I have been on a quest, rarely knowing for what.

Through choice we are able to exercise some navigational control over our lives. How often we feel as though our choices are so very limited or bleak or determined by some agenda other than our own. Even more often we make choices believing we are exercising some measure of control, when really we are just playing out the trajectory of our lifetime and the inherited focus of the soul. I learn the most about a person when I hear them talk about their path of choices which led them to the current moment.

Immersion or total involvement is one way our lives seek balance and meaning. We give ourselves over to a way of life, relationship, activity, goal to accomplish – and then completely wrap ourselves in the execution of whatever it takes to do the best we can with the choice. What happens when the choice doesn't pan out, like a marriage, a career, a lifestyle, falling short of the goal? We tend to stop immersing. We don't believe in it anymore, because it has proven to fail. It's not like we don't have things to do, it's that we no longer believe we can make a difference, because we don't really think there is a difference to be made. Nothing matters anymore, except to maintain basic life-sustaining actions that keep us appearing as though we are engaged in life.

There is a primary choice one makes – whether to be part of something or to retain an individual path. Some always need a social structure within which to identify themselves, thriving on connections that give them a sense they are engaged with outside structures. I have never found an outside structure within which to fit. I try and fail every time. Something deep inside feels stifled by the constraints. Engaging the pressures and rules of any group thinking exhausts me. I've tried, but ultimately failed, to fit into family, university, marriage, dance companies, the New York dance, performance and poetry worlds, free-lance teaching, life in Denver, the music world, politics. I was always pulling against the restraints, unwilling to accept compromises, never ready to give into feeling part of a small subculture of being human. When part of a larger group, I either cave in and neglect my individual sense of self, or I resist and eventually leave. In the midst of the pandemic, my doctor told me the extroverts were going crazy and the introverts were largely just fine. I understand a person's individual life is strengthened by union with others, but efforts often stymie me.

What happens to us is rarely even within the control of what we choose. Forced to adjust to circumstances, fate overtakes choice. We live in what was determined by past choices, but projecting the past onto the present, failing to feel what is surfacing at the moment, makes our choices weak.

4. FOCUS

So many voices to listen to – seeking resolution.

Story

I need to *re-track* my story, my own story, the unique and driven story that began (with faint glimmers of direction in Maryland and New Haven) the summer I moved to New York in 1975.

One year Dona gave me a 'past lives regression' reading with the brilliant psychic Carol Mann. I cried on and off afterwards for a couple of hours. She focused on three lives, all about coming to America from Europe – a little girl who came over on the Mayflower and soon after died, a male merchant marine who traveled back and forth from Holland, and a female Jew from Eastern Europe. She said the consistency was a struggle with the body in every case. I seemed to either get sick and die young, or work myself to death. I was never recognized for anything much in these lives, never married or had children. She told me my soul's essence is 'Divine Higher Order'. I was left with a feeling that I'd best just stop working so hard to figure life out, and keep going on my predestined purpose for higher order. She said the work of this lifetime is about letting go the urge to hurry up and get the hell out of this life, and to instead just allow it to be what it is without trying to do anything. This was experienced as increased absence and removal and further isolation. Hence, the tears. There is nothing in this 'fear-based' reality that I can relate to, and so no longer have to try to relate to any of it, but to just live with ease and grace and let go of all attachments. She gave me water and air with no other bit of history or validating information. This is the pain of my life, personified. Nothing substantive from anywhere, nothing required to do – nothing, nothing, nothing at all – no clues, no stories, no way of finding help in doing. She seemed to indicate that I already knew about most of my past lives, apparently have had many, and that the future would take care of itself if I just stopped trying to figure it all out.

And here I am still trying to figure it all out, to discover the what, how, when, where of it. I once had a room-mate who marveled at the fact the not only did I live my life, but managed to write it all down.

Broken life lines, derailed hopes and dreams, the evolution of our own personally unique story in directions we may not prefer, cause us to take refuge in the stories of others – involving ourselves in other people's lives, finding solace from pain in stories on TV, in movies, in books. When we sense our own story staggering, failing to progress, limping along on the cusp of depression and lost hope, we can easily become more invested in the stories of others, and, like a slow leak, give up the thrust, belief, and drive of our own.

I am a product of disappointment. In family, in partnership, in career. I never wanted to measure up to someone else's idea of who I could be. I never wanted to sleepwalk through tasks too stupid to warrant performing. Still I remained desperate and needy for ways to earn a living. I often fell into despair and wanted help from everyone who let me close. I patterned myself to receive that help, and became what they seemed to want me to be, losing, after time, the core of self that fed my curiosity and compelled my journey to discover how we communicate and elevate and evolve through lifetimes, past, present and future.

I have spent time letting the emotions lead entirely, which is creatively liberating, but not particularly socially progressive. I have spent time letting lessons from family lead, which caused me to race in terror into two inappropriate marriages. I have spent time trying to be all things to all people, letting whatever I perceive to be their response, determine the choice. I have let health and healing lead, enduring numerous crises of body, then afterwards identifying myself with the fact that I had survived extreme misfortune and loss, taking my lead from what that seemed to say about me.

Blind Sight

I remember a recurring dream. I was running along a dark tunnel towards a light. I could hear voices behind me, but none beside me. It felt as though the walls of the tunnel were filled with threatening sounds seeking to stop me, but I was compelled ever onward.

Like this dream, wandering through life, blind-folded, arms outstretched, touching things seemingly unrelated in order to get my bearings and continue on, the vision is impaired, the going slow and treacherous. I manage to take each step carefully and to slightly move along, but not with the force of full insight, an imbued awareness of purpose, or even a reason to continue on. Lacking vision I fly blind as a bat, afraid each step will take me into areas of pain and disaster.

But I have managed to appear to others as a sighted person, and no longer bring them into my despair or blame them for it. This, I suppose is progress, but I find very little to feed on. I want to be enlightened, mentored, led, encouraged, validated and loved. And often I simply find troubled people also trying to cope, who simply need my support. What leads a life? Where do we find clues? What to do, how to do it, when to make a choice? How do we seek inner validation?

Viola Farber, when I consulted with her about the conflicting feelings surrounding a move from Connecticut to New York responded, "I felt that way when I considered leaving the Merce

Cunningham Dance Company. You know what? I learned to see in the dark".

Output

I am clearly dedicated to keeping my work alive in the world. It is my identity and my offering, after all. The reception from those who might support it in the larger world has not been particularly forthcoming. That rare and golden moment, if it came at all, passed without my being ready to engage it and take full advantage. Now I have become obscure and hidden to all but the few who still recognize me, but who have also mostly moved on, where their careers are supported or their lives have evolved. I remain increasingly dependent on the generosity and good will of those few who still believe in me. Someone once said, when speaking of Viola Farber, "she never could catch a break". She was my most treasured dance teacher and I miss her presence on the planet.

Feelings hold me, contain me for a time in their swirling all-encompassing vertigo. I am like one of Samuel Becket's characters, the body encased in an enormous vase with only the head sticking out. Eventually the free mind works within the encasing emotion and extricates the rest of the body. This is my personal route to sanity. I seem unable to avoid repeated imprisoned states, but have become proficient at periodically breaking free of the vessel and carrying on, having absorbed the stasis of encasement, using it as food for future hope.

I'm still looking for that autonomous 'life of one's own', where I am interacting every day with more than self, with others performing actions that gather the past and, through present choices, project into the future a plan, a concept, a way of continuing together in offering to the world – the work. A difficult and strange process.

5. HELPING OURSELVES

You can't get there from there.
You can only get there by being here
and moving towards there.
But you can't GET here
if you're always wishing you were there
and you can't BE here
until you let go trying to be there,
neglecting being here.

Finding Acceptance

We are nearly at the end of another season. Time has lost its urgency. I seem to endure the days and celebrate the moments with increasing good nature and clarity. The drive to work sometimes limits my ability to breathe easily, and I sense a rumbling rise of resistance as my shoulders stoop and my resolve weakens and I wonder if I have what it takes to continue doing what I intend to do, what I say I am doing, since there is so much to do and many demands.

In seeking to find my life, I seem to have lost it. Is it necessary to lose it completely in order to find it again? As a wise person once told me "the only way out of this world is to dive into it – you find the future in committing to the present". We find clues to the next choice in the depth and scope of what is currently happening. While cultivating a growing awareness of what needs doing, we release our grip on what might have been.

It's a practice – giving over to belief over plan, action over fatigue, hope over fear, to let go of any ideal image of how we look, fit in, and manage to cope with a difficult and multi-faceted life in an attempt to find order. Feeling left out has mainly to do with investment in being included, and from the deepest perspective it doesn't really matter and has very little to do with what it is we are to do, what it is we have done, or what it is at all.

Each of us has a fantasy world that protects us from being crushed by too much of what is real. We seek escape from uncertainties and block out everything we perceive as threatening to our survival. We can only really change when the core is strengthened and the fears abate. Looking squarely at what we may do or may not do to make our journey easier, is a great challenge.

Life in the professional world seems to be a lot about managing insanity – your own (enough to keep it real) and the ones you find along the way. The point is to process information and then act to your own best advantage, suppressing impulsive alienating reactions. Try to create responses that validate the other person but in no way challenge their ego, while at the same time making sure you get what you want from them. Let go of the idea of a self that others see in you or might want you to be, seeking instead an ability to access a visionary mind, an over-mind, towards living really well in the moment as part of something much larger.

Release

Sometimes, when I am engaged in an activity that fully consumes me, I forget about what persists in plaguing me. My sense of helplessness and fear in the face of remembered pain is numbed for a time. I let go of the shock of 9/11, the disappointment in marriage, the loneliness of my life in New York, the loss of physical hardiness, the difficulty breathing, the confusion of identity as artist, the chronic economic insecurity and inability to find a way out of it. When becoming totally engrossed in a piece of writing or preparation for performance, I discover the blessed peace that accompanies work, a sense of purpose.

Tasks are accomplished, not by the act of doing, but by the impulse and focus to do. We accomplish very little when we feel under physical attack through poor health, or are otherwise processing some sort of loss and disappointment, creating a crippling sense of need.

We celebrate the incidental bounties that come our way. I found a ten dollar bill lost irretrievably in the wet gutter crossing 6th Ave. I receive $200 a month in food stamps which, when I shop the specials is more than enough to feed me really well. My stabilized rent recieves SCRIE reducing it to $410 a month for life. I have learned a kind of yoga that, if practiced regularly, keeps my body largely pain free. I have obtained and designed a wardrobe with very little expense, that assures me looking great in comfort wherever I go. I have equipment with which to execute writing and music and photographs and yoga and cooking and travelling and communication. I have a living unit that provides all the basic necessities and, although it requires lots of tweaking and upkeep, is as comfortable and nurturing as one might hope given my circumstances – my walk-up customized cave for the less than agile.

Focus on what is possible, engage with those who care, do the work before you to do, and appreciate it all.

6. TAKING STEPS

*Is there a way to go about life
that might bring us closer to some natural concept of God?*

Application

The Dalai Lama suggests having compassion for others leads directly to maintaining a calm mind which then, in turn, allows one to see reality more clearly. It's as though if one is confused with difficulties and the challenges of life, one can simply feel compassion – and the transition of calm mind to clear reality naturally follows. I love that!

Long talk with a friend about emotional transference and the way people live through the feelings of others rather than copping to their own – the delicate and difficult art of emotional differentiation.

Many years ago my close friendship with Dona was under stress, so I proposed that we have a 'dangerous conversation'. Since then it has become one of the standards of friendship to be able to talk directly to someone we trust, and say things that may be difficult, even things that may threaten the relationship entirely. We can't practice this with everyone, because some things are not ready to say and some feelings are still too raw, but I find it an incredibly useful way to experience some semblance of a meeting of truth between those who care for one another.

Perception

Since all lives are interwoven, it is necessary to validate and express our opinions, as we seek to find the difference between useful choices and those that perpetuate difficulty. Unfortunately our opinions can be perceived as judgment. This is a great dilemma of our time. Differing opinions lead to conflict and, over time, turn to division and alienation. We can only avoid these traps if we become aware and clear about how we choose to navigate the world.

What is the difference between 'judgment' and 'perception'? How can we know how to make choices about anything or anybody unless we attempt to clearly see what is going on, to weigh the options? Judgment comes when behavior or situations deeply touch our feelings giving rise to fear and anger – and everything affects feelings, even when we are detached.

There is a great difference between reactive behavior (allowing outside influences to lead the action) and proactive behavior (having a chosen center of focus that leads the action). In our current politics of lies, reaction often becomes a bullying proaction of propaganda, further confusing distinctions. We need to agree on shared truth in order to move forward. Only in kindly letting someone know how their behavior affects us can we forge a conversation. It need not be indignant or generated out of a sense of wounding. It need only be honest, but from the best part of oneself – free from any predetermined fault and disappointment.

Challenge

All kinds of pain (physical, emotional or mental) can be an early warning system leading us to alter our choices in an attempt to ease or erase the pain.

Native American cultures elevated tolerance for pain to a high level of human evolution. In spite of the awful discrimination they continue to experience, they have kept their culture alive and may become our best hope for the future of the planet.

We have to be very careful to stop trying to be in the world in ways already outgrown, and begin to be in the world in ways that return us to an active self that lives through sharing vital and lively energy with those who continue to meet us and inspire living more fully, with a greater sense of achievement and a burgeoning hope that dreams can still be realized.

It occurs to me that using our technology is like nurturing any other relationship, the more you get into it and rely on it, the more complicated it becomes. One must invest without losing oneself, just like with a human partner.

I have moved irretrievably to another side, no longer hypnotized and wooed by energies that seek to bring me down. I will not only survive, I will do it in flagrant and damaging fashion to evil powers. I am the present and everything I do manifests a future, at war in opposition to any attempts to limit, humiliate, define. I will no longer be victimized by weak powers that have no validity. I will find my own force, maintain my own balance and attempt to make a considerable contribution before my time is up.

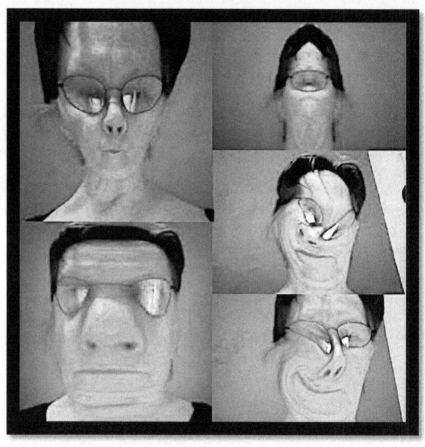

59. *CONFLICTING POV (digital photo collage) j.r-l.*

V. FROGGY THE GREMLIN

*those little moves
closer to people*

1. KNOWING OTHERS

Letting people into your life
confuses all the confidence of solitude.

Involvement

Solitude, though useful, does not replace our need for friends – actual chosen people, not just family, with whom we exchange time and space and share a sense of the present. Some we have know for many years, some we find along the way, and are touched by them. Forging these relationships becomes our pathway through life. People scrape against us with healing contact but also another kind of touch that can wound.

I have often made poor choices of 'who to get close to'. Besides two failed marriages, there have been numerous love affairs, friends as peers, work partners, playmates. Fragile when it comes to interaction, I have been easily confused about how people come together to create an illusion of reality they can agree on, resulting in support for one another, a mutual and shared agreement bringing more hope than trouble, each willing to pay the dues of required attention and necessary investments of time and money.

In many relationships my ability to *differentiate* has been late in developing. We have to know the difference between ourselves and the other. Individuals who actually know themselves generate a level of trustworthiness. Only in present encounters can we make choices, each contact bringing its own truths and pitfalls. There's a need to know how the *other* is feeling about the way life is going together. Difficult conversations ensue.

If you are lucky, you will find people who truly value you. Sharing past intensities may or may not have been a mutually positive experience. It's essential to be open and honest when you are confused about behavior, but it is also important to accept whatever someone offers, when they are able to offer it. Considering the other's point of view is essential – proving you value their individuation from you, their choices in regards to you, and the belief you share a mutual trust. When that trust appears to be broken, it's necessary to speak up. *Thinking* it is broken is often not the truth of the matter. We can imagine so many responses that prove to be simply wrong. We can't know the mind of another, or whether they truly value you or not. We gain their trust by behavior that validates and trusts them, reaping what we sow.

Vampires

Some folks are really clever, capable of deeply undercutting you, extracting what they need, regardless of what the surface seems to show. These are often highly intelligent people who never really found a listening, nurturing self to offer others. They feign deep interest, ask for your opinion, but then (with what seems like an unconscious determination) refute any view offered – wanting to get close, taking and then rejecting, later perhaps proffering it as their own.

I never learned how to disempower these sorts of folks – or to leave them alone. They have moved through my life like farm machinery, threshing their harmful way destroying my confidence and taking advantage of my open invitations. They go in for the kill and then you are shocked and surprised to find yourself under-mined by their duplicity, feeling so completely depleted and weakened by such allowed blood-letting experiences. I wonder if one can become immune to these sucking affects and protect oneself from getting hurt, perhaps by being more and more mindful of just what is going down in these flawed human exercises with which we engage, just to stay part of some reality, even when it turns out to be a ruse?

Other people are a constant challenge to our ability to protect our own vulnerable and fragile selves.

Competition

We need to let go of everything we think about comparison and climb inside our own life, enjoying the ride.

Competitive parallel lives push me to places I prefer not to go. Perhaps I believe too much in the fate of the individual unrestricted by a desire to please. We battle professional demands to accumulate names of recognizable note, having the effect of bringing us an acceptable measure of *success*, as we drop those names. Society continues to demand we prove ourselves worthy by requiring proof of association.

Closeness

It seems as though it is often our dysfunctions that bring us together, but it's also those same dysfunctions that pull us apart and keep us from getting closer. Enjoying drinking together can lead to chronic alcoholism. Addiction of any kind is anti-relationship.

When, as a child, a person doesn't experience the receiving of love, whether or not they may actually be truly loved, they spend their lives looking for it. This can become severe dissociative behavior, resulting in a lifelong battle. Distracted by what we want and do not have, we lose our inner focus of validity, giving over to the impression that our lack is a comment on our worth, making us extremely sensitive to being criticized by those closest to us, especially family.

Close friendships are about love, respect, joy, shared pain, no judgment, and regular inquiry as to the way things are going. We learn from this sort of exchange, as long as we listen as much as share. All friends really want to hear is that we are well, active, positive and working. When we don't feel these things we fail to share and become numb. There can be old sensations of unbearable loss, and a reluctance to make the effort to connect, because we don't feel strong and neutral enough to be with people.

Interaction

Don't bemoan your choices, honor your choices – and let go those things you might regret. I regret I wasn't in better psychological shape when I was receiving attention for my work in the late 80's. Instead, in a misguided search for love, I ended up investing in too many relationships that offered little good for me. I could never figure out who to trust, how to trust them, what to trust them with. It was decades of taking a stand after being hurt, only allowing the very few in. I missed years of solidifying chances for enduring friendships. Navigating myself through career waters was a dicey trip.

I mourn the loss of some friendships. With many it was a matter of my not being able to keep up with demands of the times – like never being able to afford travel, restaurants and shows out in the world, especially while recovering from poor health and then observing pandemic rules. Blessedly I still rely on a handful of close confidants who 'keep me on the planet' – reliable friends, who frequently lend support and encouragement, many of whom live far away. All have very active lives where I am only sometimes included. They offer economic lifts from time to time and essential emotional support, often showing they still believe in me. Extremely grateful for each one, I remain in awe of all human exchanges that luckily come my way, though the older we get, the more we lose.

2. CONTRASTS

Haunted by themes of unrequited love
in an environment of massive doubt and mortal illness.

Our Sexes

We are all caught in a sexually insecure culture, often revealed as sexual exhibitionism, permissiveness or repression – a lot of acting out. In coping, we create strong identifiers – straight, bi-sexual, homosexual, gay, lesbian, transvestite, transsexual, non-binary, queer, cis gender, polyamorous, panromantic, asexual and other emerging categories, attempting to define and codify our varied individual relationship to sex. Human evolution has encouraged choice to determine destiny.

I never had much success with sex or romantic love. After moving to New York City in 1975 in my early 30's, I was a bit wild, experimented rather recklessly, always ending up emotionally devastated when it was clear there was nothing more there than sex. I fell with my heart and often landed on it, unable to separate my body from what I was feeling. Closing down sexually has been my response. I have always thought I am largely asexual, never finding sex that interesting a subject or activity. With few exceptions, it was often messy, led more to discomfort than joy – and rarely worth all the fuss. Didn't engage my own sexuality until I had left two unsatisfying marriages – the first to a closeted homosexual with a penchant towards alcoholism, the second to a confessed transvestite, who later realized his transsexual desire and, after the age of 60, underwent the brave and difficult surgical transition of becoming a woman.

More than mere procreation, perhaps it is the dichotomy of difference, the need to possess another that drives human coupling, led by an innate impulse to partner. Variations serve to make the search more interesting, more open, more free.

We often exhibit a tendency to predict, desire, intellectualize a chosen outcome of relationship before the relationship has even begun, based not in what passes between two people that is new and unique and individual to each person, but based in past experience, perceived wants, and especially in protective attitudes that serve to shield us from emotional and sexual exchanges that may prove hurtful or at best challenging and confusing.

I applaud the opening of sexual norms. A society's acceptance of choices thought in the past to be deviant, brings us all closer to harmony and peace with the realization that love, not sex, is the guiding human principle to cultivate with others. Union with the other remains a mystery, no matter what the sexual parameters may be.

Our Emotions

Humans have traded sexual repression for emotional repression. As our sexuality slowly became liberated from the religious strictures that dominated our founding, and as Freud's subversion of the emotions into an entirely sexual cause took root, we found our lives dominated by body in the service of brainless hormones. Losing the ability to completely feel an entire range of emotional responses to living with other humans, we became less and less available. It is inconvenient to *feel* too much. We become vulnerable to the ways in which the feelings of others affect us, and must adapt constantly to what we are being presented. Those who remain emotionally repressed, who deny their feelings even exist and have great difficulty owning them, are, ironically, owned by them. Most often it is feelings of anger and fear that take deep root and define being.

125

Communication breaks down and everybody loses. Confused about the actions of others, a person becomes critical of them, denying they may have cause and unwilling to see that cause. They remain unable to help that person see into themselves through relationship, which might happily result in some sort of mutual understanding.

Bad feelings are as easily shared as good feelings. If someone feels bad, it is probably because someone else feels bad in response to perceived behavior and simply returns the gift. Feelings represent a contagion. We all have the power to generate good feelings or bad. Nobody wants to accept responsibility for failure to engage or an inability to be reliably present, so we just make excuses garnering more bad feelings. Caring for those who consistently fail us brings unexpected despair and pain. Partnering with depression is most difficult where a habit of withholding has become entrenched.

Relationships shift and change over the decades of a life. When a teenager, one is always looking for the next exciting person who will bring forth new feelings and sensations of attraction, lust, love, romance, intimacy. In their 20's one begins to search for that one particular person to share all the best of what being with another can mean. Then in the 30's there is a kind of desperation to find intimate friends with whom to find a future, and that desperation only grows in the 40's. Quick attraction and quick rejection typifies these decades of searching, finding, losing, giving up and yearning. When one hits the 50's one becomes truly glad for all the people who seem to have survived the relationship wars and begins to value all friendly relationships with a renewed appreciation and care. And by the time one is into the 60's, the remaining close people become incredibly valued, even though there are far fewer than ever before. Once one hits the 70's there is a daunting awareness of accumulative loss.

Emotional engagement brings out the creative. Tension feeds us, drives us to explore and understand surges of feelings that take us by surprise, irrational pushes and pulls of the human heart realizing the deep need of all people to be loved and cared for.

What makes friendship? Loyalty over time, showing up, learning how to be with, easily. Then there are the conversations, dangerous or not, that guide our choices and determine ways to navigate towards a deepening shared understanding of the other and a resultant growing confidence in one's self. It sounds so simple and really is, but we frequently try and miss, as so many people flow through the gathering colander of life and are drained away.

In the past, I would assume closeness when it wasn't shared. Now I try to be my kindest self, respond to the other in the most respectful, honest and sensitive way possible, rarely desiring more than what is easily forthcoming. Whatever develops is what it becomes. Wanting more, too often proves painful.

3. ENCOUNTERS

Understanding uncomfortable moments shared.

Power

Shouting argument on the street at St. Mark's Place about politics. He is a right wing war-mongering advocate. I just couldn't deal with his insistence of certainty. He claims that, because he has read all available world history, he knows more than anybody else, and anybody who thinks differently from him only does so because they are not as informed as he. Later he called to apologize and even hinted that he realized he is emotionally invested in these opinions and it has intruded on his position at work.

This conflict leads me to think about how and why *politics* is such a volatile conversational subject. I suspect it has to do with power and the will to power. A person's politics tells everything about them in terms of what they believe about power and how it is acquired and wielded in the world, especially about how one seeks power over others. This is why the subject is so heated – especially between men and women.

It also occurs to me that he is invested in history as the source of what to think about the present, and strongly believes that we are doomed to play out our history based completely on what has gone before. I believe history teaches us what to avoid. Changes come from seeing the present from a fresh eye, from enlightened points of view, from a sense that the world can be changed and the balance of power can be affected.

Judgment

He is withdrawn, unavailable, a non-present cipher who only seems to light up and thrive when he is being focused on by her. She is his conduit to the world and bears this burden as though it is her due.

He sits as an observer and, when he perceives something he doesn't like, or he suspects reflects badly on the person he is with, or, in association, on him, he registers the judgment but says nothing. This results in bad feelings never confronted or exposed, so never released. They build up and get between people.

On the surface he has adopted an attitude of complete validation and acceptance of everything that exists in direct relation to him, having invested his total being in what he has surrounded himself with. Any criticism or disagreement he takes as a direct attack and responds with passive aggression, the way humans often deny truth. In some ways he can't hear the emotional reality of another person, and, when unavoidably exposed to it, he just shuts down and removes himself completely.

This inability to deal with the reality of conflict at the moment it occurs, thinking it is an elevated choice to ignore it, pretend it isn't there, refusing to deal with the full impact of perceived reality, reveals his limitations and that must make him very uncomfortable.

He talks at me, as though he just needs a sounding board in order to better hear himself. Incapable of interactive conversation, countering most comments with competitive ammunition remarks, there was no sense of being happy in someone else's good fortune, an appreciation of common ground or even a sharing of thoughts or ideas.

Differentiation

He is undifferentiated. He has never learned the difference between himself and the other. He has to relate experiences through himself before he can even come close to seeing or hearing another person. He thinks someone else's shortcomings reflect badly on him, so he distances himself from them in order to disassociate with something that, at the root, he has no real ability to understand. He reveals no strong sense of *other*. He really doesn't know what another *is*. He grows puzzled when someone wants him to listen and see them, because he just isn't capable of doing so without first filtering their being through his own experience in order to actually perceive what he is being given, or asked, or challenged by. When he perceives someone has wants or needs or difficulties, he first tries to identify with them, and when he fails to understand in terms of himself, he distances himself from them entirely. This inability to differentiate reveals a deeper problem, that he doesn't actually believe he exists, and he has to use everything touching him to prove to himself that he does. He is actually completely distanced from himself. A person unable to realize that they are they and the other is the other, can never have a relationship, because all their relationships are with themselves, and that is ultimately unsatisfying.

Suffering

There is some kind of depleting that she undergoes as she engages in her life, and is often simply unavailable. I seem to further stress her out, as though what I need from her is more than she can bear. She has become some sort of cipher for what is wrong with the world, and validates herself in this attitude that life is difficult and stressful and out to get her.

I suspect some of what I experienced with her was that lack of showing her my suffering. She is wired to support and improve lives that are close to her and to celebrate those who overcome great adversity. When I present groomed and well-dressed and capable of dealing, she doesn't have that much to do and it seems to confuse her. There was a 'weighing and measuring' of me and the result was puzzlement rather than clarity. She has found a level of support that suits her. She seems to know how to support the lives of others, but is still confused about how to create her own.

Traps

Have reached a frame of mind where I no longer think I may be one of the good guys, but could be considered part of the problem. My choices throughout life have always been self-serving. I remain highly critical of those who seem to exhibit traits that are odious and contrary to what I deem as good in the world. I admire those who speak truth to power and put quality work out, but dismiss those who seem wooed by their own rhetoric and are riding an undeserved wave of celebrated popularity.

4. PARTNERS

love's a verb
an action word
steered by surprise
sticking together
shared surmise

Finding

Sometimes we don't marry the love of our life because the one we love does! I have habitually fallen in love with unavailable men.

I married twice, believing each saw my inner glow and valued my strengths. Because they were confused, in their own way, and I was also confused, we each believed we needed an *other* to go against, to complete us. In those marriages, I slowly became less and less of myself and more and more in service to shared confusion.

There are many ways of loving. We are restricted by our own inherent limitations and by the methods with which we navigate our journey. We all have ways, when close, of making a person feel bad about themselves, partly to keep them from swallowing us.

I keep trying to find out what can be known, feeding the *unknown*, discovering what is inherently new. I regret I am not someone capable of weaving a mystery of magical thinking instead of intensely trying to figure out a dynamic based in truth that has its own trajectory.

Finding trusted and reliable friends and soul-mates takes a lot of trial and error.

The fact that there has been no love story in my life – no actual, lived one – leads me to believe I have shot way past the target and have failed to follow my own rules for living. I kept trying, but have repeatedly failed to nurture love.

Bridges

You become a jewel in the setting of my recent history. We agree to create a bridge, a pathway between us. I throw something out onto the bridge. You access the bridge, grab what is thrown, and then scurry back to your side, leaving the bridge empty. I cross the bridge and whack you. I throw something out onto our bridge and you move towards it, luring me out from my side to meet you and share in what is there. We each return to our side without the need to whack. What can you throw onto the bridge that we can share while there? And is there a way of making the bridge feel tangible and present when we aren't playing on it? I seek a new clarity, not a replay of ancient games.

Security

Memory swings back and forth between what we hear, feel, understand, do, do not do, constantly juggling fear and anger, two negative emotions feeding on one another.

I'm thinking about the inadequacy of conversation, We ask questions and share opinions about what is going on around us, about what feeds us, impedes us, the struggles we invent and endure. It can be enlightening, but is often tedious.

You ask what it is that keeps marriages ongoing, families sustaining years of difficult interactions and life experience together? Beyond the point that every individual situation is different, and that there is a larger plan for each of us, the process could be: undeniable attraction, mutual action sustaining that attraction, investing in the creation of a dialog that can negotiate individual need, inevitable change, shared use, improving a mutual process that facilitates acting on unknowable truths and undeniable urges, caring more about what you create together than what you have alone, letting go, appreciating what endures in the larger picture, showing up and honoring the power of memory.

It really is a matter of degrees of encouragement. One is more inclined to get out into the world and interact with it when one is semi-secure at home.

60. *EXPLODING SKIES* *(digital photo collage) j.r-l.*

VI. HUNTRESS

seeking balance
in an off-kilter world

1. LOCATION, LOCATION, LOCATION

piles collecting
dust balls scurry
environment says
clean with a fury
stuff is blocking
up the action
lack of motion
sick reaction
our voice is calm
no constant yelping
spontaneity
is helping
life invites
a daily reckoning
participation
always beckoning
goals beyond
not yet revealed
but ears are open
eyes peeled.

Disarray

We often find ourselves living or working in an environment that has evolved to hold us back, throwing clutter and an excess of things in the way of moving to action. Cutting back on belongings is necessarily based on a clear structuring of a life to cut to, which is not always so obvious. We need to know more clearly who we are and what we are up to. Launching into a sorting process can help us discover those things, noting that our desire to limit choices is often in conflict with a desire to access endless ones.

We can also be well served by the periodic choice to retreat, taking time to go deeply inside in a search to perhaps discover truth of existence, endurance and cause, reinvesting in mind and body. Retreat can be a great help to proceeding with the clearing process. Once in retreat we are faced with our collected chaos. We open space, make room, introduce more chaos. We attempt to establish a living and working place where the function of systems, learned and mastered, can handle daily bits that have been obtained, attracted and included. We seek a procedure for processing *complex chaos* not only in our own space, but as we see the world.

Objects and ideas surround us, feeding our muses and immersing us in an environment of possibility. Moments pass without stress or pressure, but with a sense of poise in purpose and clarity of intention. We reintegrate everything at hand, organize it for work, keeping daily needs and changes easily accessed, weighing validity or value in this changing existence, enjoying the details.

This is contented anonymity. Needing the calm and freedom of time and environment as it changes within us, on us, through us, beside us and in spite of us.

Structures

One must come up with structures that serve choices in lifestyle, and then provide consistent maintenance of those structures. It's like you have to create the patterns of your life, and then practice those patterns. We often fail in the attempt to maintain, or have so many structures and patterns that have been proven, we barely find time to practice them all, but we are all desperately in need of structures that bridge our ideas and choices with the larger world.

I am a 'systems analyst'. I delight in figuring out detailed ways to make things more efficient and useful. I love abstract structures that include ways of addressing space and time, threaded through by clues and ideas about how specific moments occur within the structure. I don't really know how to do anything that conforms to pre-existing forms, since I prefer to create new ones. I am always trying to improve the situation, make it more comfortable, useful, contained, prepared. I tend to keep and honor things that have brought my life a certain meaning.

Models

Sometimes there is a need to have some sort of paradigm, an existing model upon which to base our choices. The best role models are those we have observed, often over years, who seem to navigate this world of change and choice and find some validation along the way. I always enjoy the chance to visit the homes of people I like.

Visitors have said my home is a living installation. Seeing the way others organize their lives is not only instructive, but fascinating, like the way our Zoom lives reveal a chosen frame of environment.

Just how do we maneuver and make distinctions, exercise our choices, easily relate through them? I am alarmed and dismayed by some lifestyles I witness, often living examples of how people get in their own way. Those who are aggressively competitive for instance, present as overly-confident, ego-centered and desperate, where certainty and lack of doubt presents as rigidity.

To know yourself, requires a lifetime of response to change and a willingness to take chances. Embracing the *other* includes hearing what they have to say but taking none of it personally. More than constant, blatant validation this requires the ability to differ, express a contrasting opinion or observation, and to differentiate oneself comfortably without fear of loss.

Overcoming Inertia

There are strong resistances operating on our resolve: emotional turmoil, physical and economic insecurity; desire to satisfy needs, however trivial or mundane; fear of falling into complete madness. It is often difficult to perceive what is offered without risking being engulfed by it. When one sequesters too much, one risks developing an inflated ego, as if our concerns were really all that important in the larger scheme of things.

To make contact with other souls, those with whom we do not live or work; to reach out to an unknown cosmos of being with a developed process of working; to catch a toehold upon which to land when falling; to learn about doing through the creation of a moment in time which can be held, remembered and shared – these are some quality tasks before us.

We need to feel free to be the way we are, without trying to control the other person's perception of us – it's just too damned self-conscious that way. Let the other person deal with your truth of the moment and see reality passing as it is, rather than denying inconvenient or uncomfortable truths in a vain attempt to predict outcomes.

2. CITY VS. NATURE

Celestial events of moon and sun
vistas of mountains, forests of trees
sounds of birds, coastlines of seas
healing
whatever the weather.

Shame

Brad was speaking of reading Anna Karenina again and how one of the characters expressed feelings of the change between country and city and how in the city they felt 'shame'. Could it have to do with millions of open agendas flying around everywhere in the city, emanating from individuals who are drawn to the city in hopes of gaining some sort of power in the world? In the country your measure of power is nature and nature is integral to survival. In the city one seeks survival regardless of any aspect of nature unless it is a huge storm, powerful enough to get the attention of the millions doggedly pursuing their ends with blinders up, defenses in place and weapons at the ready.

So we arrive in the city with our spirits full, our bodies fit, and our souls satisfied, only to be confronted with a swirling vortex of 'floating agendas' which can so easily catch us up, push us out, or fail to see us at all. And there is often 'shame' in our experience, knowing that, in the city, presumed goals are constantly moving and changing. Validation, often existing just beyond our grasp, is seen to be carried off by those we may consider lesser recipients of the rewards of human achievement. Our sense of our own humanity becomes judged, not by our own values, but by the values of others. In this instance, when our inner validation is compromised or damaged, the city can be an awful place to live.

Separation Anxiety

When asked in a 1972 radio interview "what did I like about he city" I said "living in New York is like living everywhere in the world all at once". So I have thrown my advantages into life in the city, even as people I like leave town and desert what the city offers.

Going out for basic errands, I become further isolated and see mainly the young, the competitive, the driven, managing to spend required money to endure the physical assault of a city environment.

My skills at career planning in the New York City art world always seem to come up short, and most of my ideas cost money, few make it. I have spent some time visiting people who have found life in a gentler environment – in Santa Fe, in Ocean Grove, in Vermont. The city has its charms, but time in nature tunes my voice and leads me on and feeds the soul healing the spirit, opening my mind to what is yet to come.

Understanding this conundrum I continue to live in my affordable, customized, walk-up New York City cave for the less than agile. There is a strange dichotomy between what the universe has provided for me in terms of a place to live within the confines of a limited social security income, and what I may need in order to feel the life flow more strongly, namely access to nature and the simplicity of a lifestyle structured around the natural world.

Sanctuary

Sometimes, just being away from home and into nature for a time will bring us back to balance and we are able to get past ourselves and down to work. I resist going out on the street, but am happy to report that my apartment is blissfully quiet, and the work energies begin to move through me as soon as I return home. Here are the basic tools to move all my lifelong output of work and thought, along with basic life sustaining amenities. I am fed by this gift of fortunate sanctuary.

3. PUZZLES

Virtual time conspires against us,
unable to get clear about actual time.

Remaining in touch with what's happening all over the world from differing points of view can be very humbling.

One person's idea of 'trouble' is another person's way of exercising 'rigor'.

I communicate confidence when I focus more on presence than on presentation.

What is truth in one instance, fails to be true in another. We struggle to find consistency. Addressing change is often more powerful than maintaining consistency.

Ben Kingsley says that those who create also heal, and creative people are fragile, so must surround themselves with those in whom they place absolute trust. If we surround ourselves with those who do not offer trust, we are drained and unable to be fully creative.

There was a survey on the radio – if you had to give up one of the 5 senses (sight, hearing, touch, taste, smell) which one would it be? Most people said they would give up smell. Smell seems the most mysterious to me as it evokes memories like no other sense. Taste is the one I would forego. It is delicious and sensuous but not as clear a guide as seeing, hearing, touching and smelling. To taste is an inner experience, lovely and powerful, but not the most essential to dealing with the world of physical reality.

When you organize your life around a very strongly held belief system, you risk collapsing as a human being if life and the world proves those beliefs to be corrupt, corruptible and false. This is true for politics, religion, career, and inherited value systems.

We are part of history if we focus on being part of a present that cannot know it's place in history. Being *fully engaged* in what is happening speaks more eloquently to the future, than being *aware* of how what is happening may impact the future.

The world gets smaller and civilizations collide. We grow up, grow older, grow into our spirits, pause in the struggling, think of how many kindnesses, over all the years, we have received. The names that surface are those we have a certain connection with, those who help keep us on the planet, those who are part of the weave of our life.

61. TEXTURES *(digital photo collage)* j.r–l.

VII. JAW TALK

*interactions
with global spinning*

1. FINAL ANSWERS

You can't run from death,
but you want to be ready when you go.

Family Matters

In 2002, my older sister Lyn (who suffered from multiple sclerosis) went out with her friends in Denver, dressed as a tiger, to celebrate Halloween and her birthday. The next day, November 1st, the day she was born in 1938, she committed suicide with the help of a right to die organization called The Hemlock Society. The years and months leading up to this decision and act were stressful, amazing, filled with love and sibling struggles. Both our parents had passed and she was my only sibling. I supported her choice as others fought her on it. One distant cousin actually told her she would burn in hell and then rebuked me "in the name of Jesus" for my support. But she was already nearly wheel chair bound, and had always been a very independent spirit. She just wasn't going to face years of slowly losing function while remaining alive in an assisted care situation. She was a very determined Scorpio and her act was reasoned, generous and brave.

I think about Lyn and our Lay family Christmases and feel guilty about my own desires and lack of perspective when growing up. My vanity and desperation to present myself well, overshadowed deeper thoughts. I struggled to escape rather than to feed and validate. Consumerism was the seasonal guide, even though we never had the means to go overboard, and Daddy's views never got expressed or lived out unless it was in his music. I cried when I heard the radio story of the Hard Corps Chorale that some soldiers created in Iraq, singing carols in Saddam Hussein's palace, thinking that was something Daddy would have done. I do think it was the Navy that encouraged his alcoholism, after all, and a sad sense that he had married into the wrong family. But he was so anxious to please, to be validated, accepted, make a go of anything on his own, that he caved in from need of outside validation, receiving so little from inside the family. I loved him more than I ever knew, more than he may ever have known. Perhaps he knows it now. When he passed I felt an amazingly strong surge in energy, as though he were now somewhere he could truly help me.

I really miss Lyn in the world although I am resisting writing about her life and suicide. I know there is a story there, but I am loathe to go into it for fear of losing myself in the same way I was afraid I might lose myself if I went to see her one last time. It is my greatest fear to be weighed, measured, judged and found wanting, totally losing myself. This fear limits my choices and regulates certain protective behaviors.

I can allow her to find her place in the family grouping of those who have passed. Such a small, tight, limiting family group. There were the primary four of us. My mother (I rarely called her Mother, just Mom) and father whom I never called Dad, always Daddy. Dad was reserved for Gramp (the nickname for my Grandfather, her father). Mom covered up her insecurity with stubbornness and a sort of hard inability to accept and flow. She never was quite able to assert herself, so developed this cold way of coping in order to get some of what she needed. Daddy, on the other hand, never seemed to be capable of getting anything of value from the world and was easily taken in by those less talented and honest than he. And as for the family, all were swamped by the alpha personality of the gifted and powerful father figure of Gramp, the doctor, the paycheck, the fixer, the one everyone turned to when things went badly, but the one who seemed incapable of teaching his children self-reliance and to impart to them the confidence to be themselves and find a valid way in the world. His way was to leave well enough alone and spend his energies enjoying his golf game, his financial independence, and his grandchildren – until things went sour – then he swooped in and took care of everyone as well as he knew how. And that was usually far better than they were able to take care of themselves. Living to the age of 95 he would say it was liberating to get old because one doesn't have to be tactful anymore.

I seem to be the repository of this strange legacy of family that lived and died following some sort of sold or stolen dream that was represented, in the larger picture, by Dr. Earle Cleveland Haas and his invention of Tampax, the most interesting part of our story in terms of American family history. I did that work in my Bessie

142

award winning performance *The Grandfather Tapes 1985* – where he told his life story in an edited recorded interview, juxtaposed by the path upon which I have found myself.

Last night the heart went wild and I actually thought I might die in my sleep, so I sat at the desk and wrote a note to 'whomever' as to closing off my 'affairs'. I have been lax about following through on a death plan. Except for Dona agreeing to be my person who decides when to pull the plug in the event of incapacitation, I haven't dealt with how to handle everything else.

Very strange how calmly I accepted the fact that I might soon join those who have gone before.

Magical Thinking

I often quote The Desiderata, a long meditative poem written in the 1920's. One line says "Take kindly the counsel of the years, gracefully surrendering the things of youth". I know folks who refuse to adjust to adverse circumstances, living in some kind of magical thinking that bad news can be ignored and they will never have to process or come to grips with looming illness or their own demise. I wish we might all look upon aging as a stage of life to be honored, not avoided. Too often we get caught up in denying the truth of our own mortality and, instead of moving through illness and infirmity with acceptance, we resist, struggle and fight to the end. I hope for an easy death, where I am able to embrace the inevitable and go out gently and easily, as did Helen Manfredi at the age of 102, my aunt Ren Lay at 104, and choreographer David Gordon at 86. Bless them for leading the way.

I think of Oliver Sachs who wrote this about facing his final journey: "My predominant feeling is one of gratitude. I have loved and been loved. I have been given much and I have given something in return. Above all, I have been a sentient being, a thinking animal, on this beautiful planet, and that in itself has been an enormous privilege and adventure".

Pain in the Moment

Pain only exists in the moment. There is no real memory of pain – only the helplessness one feels while enduring it, and the fear it will return. This is why victims of torture and physical trauma develop post-traumatic stress disorder – because the damage done by an experience and endurance of pain – especially over long periods of time – is remembered in the psyche and that is where it continues to damage us.

While on retreat in Santa Fe, staying at a guest cottage away from everything, I woke up at 2:10 am with screaming pain seeming to come from every joint in my body. I was crying and pleading with the powers that be as I started walking around the house, drinking water and then doing some basic stretches, completely stumped about what seems to be happening to me. It could be the bed. It could be anything, really. All I knew was it felt as though tiny devils with pitchforks were running around sticking them into my joints. The pain seemed to encompass my entire body, and I was trying everything I knew to do to purge whatever this was from my system. With all the sunshine, walking, helpful company, hot baths, I seemed to be in a healing paradise, but then this hit and I felt quite incapable of bearing it. The sound of my voice pleading and moaning and vocalizing the pain was so intense, just glad I was out there all alone, hoping neighbors didn't hear.

Patience

Thick Nhat Hahn tells a story about a man whose mother died suddenly and his father was so distraught he threw all his grown children out and would not open the door. So one of the sons just went there frequently with love letters to his father and flowers leaving them on the doorstep. After a few months his father opened the door. During this time the son said he had to try to get past the feelings of rejection and understand the suffering his father must be experiencing. The mother had always been the emotional intelligence of the family and his father did not have the skills to navigate a massive ocean of grief, so he just closed off. With the

144

patient consistency of letting him know he was there and loved him, the son helped the father open the door, the door to himself.

2. NEWS-PROMPTED RANTS

Through paying attention to a larger world,
we discover shared life.

Tribes

The major flaw in the history of man's development becomes increasingly clear as we proceed over the decades. Somewhere along the way the power struggle for basic needs of food and shelter and the instinct to reproduce in order for the species to survive morphed into a world system of measurable value – money, ability to pay, worth in terms of earnings. Human lifestyle reflects this, especially in the U.S. where our choices for development serve as a harbinger of things to come in the world community. Many live for what they get out of it, what they have to show for living, i.e. material goods, wealth, power to generate more. These things, in turn, seem to determine with whom we associate. Our choices of whom to get close to begin with those we are born close to. After that, choice of companionship and comradery, mates and working partners is often a matter of an attempt to perpetuate a presumed lifestyle. Each cultural group sets parameters for belonging, but they all wrestle with individual desire for personal gain versus group survival. Needs expand as prosperity grows and choices of who to get close to are confusingly colored with family influences and degrees of competition. What feeds our shared humanity? How do we get fed and still manage to maintain individual integrity and continuity, a sense of a self with differing values from those with whom we associate?

Then there is this strange human tendency to blame someone or something 'other' for what goes wrong with our lives. If you don't 'go along' with what your peers believe, you become suspect. Pressure is on to comply to the wildest lies, sign on to the most bizarre theories, and then blame anybody who doesn't agree with you. Exploring cause seems never to go far enough in explaining or

145

solving this dilemma. Going more deeply into a problem often leads us into a morass of possibilities and a frustrating search for truths obscured by lies and believed by those who feel oppressed.

Citizens who are moderately successful support and invest in the status quo for fear they will lose if they support change. There is so little vision, so little ability for most people to see the consequences of their silent compliance, so they practice denial and acceptance which makes it easy for them to be blinded by what they perceive as irrefutable power – eventually leading to corrupt government.

Radical extremism is the scourge of our time. Repeated mass shootings, attacks on innocents at random and mob eruptions arise from a world in crisis. It is a result of the knee-jerk human reaction to blame someone else for the pain one feels. In this *blaming* mentality, acts of random and unpredictable violence occur. Choices to become the instrument of mayhem are grounded in a personal belief that one is righteous in their blame and justified to strike out – whether against another country in the name of a distorted religious or political belief, or against fellow humans because one feels powerless and wronged in their context.

The world is rife with dedicated groups. Those that possess and pretend to power are no longer the only ones that matter. There are groups espousing violence, crime, worldwide conflagration. There are groups espousing peace and philanthropy above all else. And then there are the political parties clinging to ways of subjecting populations to antiquated ways of thinking, still trying to govern the world with old ideas. There are so many groups with valid or invalid points of view, we need revolutionary thinkers to lead the way out of this growing tribalism.

Regressive American Solutions

Too many days of watching communities, beleaguered from war, criminal acts or natural disaster, share in the loss of sons and daughters to unnecessary violence, suffering in common and railing against the failure of world government, having lost everything.

We have fouled our environment perhaps beyond reclamation in order for the few at the top of the pile to accumulate wealth beyond need and to wield power over other lives which borders on enslavement. We repeatedly cede to corrupt authority the responsibility for our well-being in the world. Unless there is a grassroots attempt to believe we can once again champion democracy, all is lost. The US Constitution was a strong idea, but the people who have gained control over it have subverted all concept of freedom and their greedy, small-minded, self-interested values have got to be pointed out, named and exorcised before this country can ever hope to heal. All press that simply gives them equal time is incapable of covering the truth, unable to uncover the epidemic of lies, and is failing the American people at a time when many are losing life, home, work and hope. The strength that once was the United States has become a quickly fading dream for a peaceful and plentiful daily life, and has instead become large groups scrapping for crumbs while small groups gamble away the riches and resources of a once worthy country of citizens.

It is shocking what the fanatics have managed with inflexible, biased systems of belief. This is not a time for feinting, for the frightened or disadvantaged to bow and appease blatant crimes against our country, our planet. There must be courage and action exposing those responsible. We must dispel all attempts to validate their blundering with 'benefits of doubt'. With unrelenting focus we must expose, fight, name, and argue every lying voice that has foisted an attempted coup or perpetuates a deadly assault on the earth.

Those of you who still believe we can win by moving towards the center do not understand the fight. This is not an argument couched in leftist political rhetoric, nor is it a simple plea for a more progressive approach to governing. It is a fight for the very soul of the nation, the survival of the planet. If we are not already infected, we are susceptible. The cleverness of deceit that greets us every day in the news and in the Congress has become a powerful sickness showing no clear symptoms, making it doubly hard to combat. Clarity of focus, unity of message, consistency in action are necessary to differentiate the unifying spiritual soul from the divisive religious or racist soul. Even power brokers who see the corruption will fail in their use of opposing power unless they can also see the way tired and out-dated attempts to collaborate feed the problem. There are times when confrontation is necessary. Emperors must be seen as naked, and all attempts at compromised double dealings dispelled. We are primarily engaged in the painful job of exposing corruption, and we can't do that if we retreat into allowing wiggle room and negotiating tactics to blind us to the urgency of that daunting task – namely calling out those who have been radicalized with lies and false propaganda. There is a kind of madness loose in the world and, like in the 1930's & 40's, it must be neutralized. A drastic course correction is required.

Seditious Rumblings

It appears that there's no violation of the U. S. Constitution too heavy-handed to alarm Republican partisans who've been hiding under their collective beds since 9/11. A healthy democracy contains responsibility, transparency, and accountability. How far so many of the democracies of the world have strayed from those basic precepts, and the authoritarians are taking full advantage.

We have beome a Medieval-like world of base values, deeply opposing forces and religious fanaticism. The leading emotion, fear, gives rise to greed and righteousness, giving rise in turn to intolerance. Like serfs in the Middle Ages, we abnegate, give over rights, fail to discern truth from lies, and believe the zealots who benefit by our frozen awareness. We cried "Bush, the Protector" when the greatest attack on our homeland happened during his watch. It is unbelievable to me how brain-washed the people have become and how unscrupulous many politicians remain. I was reminded of this during a recent sleepless night because a neighbor's dog, who had been left in the hall outside its owner's apartment, was barking for hours, and the neighbor, whom I finally roused from a drunken stupor and told her what was going on, claimed I had "imagined it". If only it were true, that I have 'imagined' the 2000 election insanity, the negligent Bush stance on terrorism prior to 9/11, the lies leading us into war in Iraq, the defense secretary's faulty plan for that war and its horrific, continuing aftermath, the scandal at Abu Graib prison, the assault by the attorney general on our civil liberties, the inarticulate, simplistic leadership of a president whose military record was suspect at best, AWOL at worst, a vice president whose private corporate interests made billions on the war, a foreign policy of pre-emption that has served to alienate the world community, strengthen the terrorist threat and isolate us as a rogue nation, bent on war over peace, incapable of negotiation, compromise, understanding and thought which might elevate us into the future as a viable partner in global concerns. And that was all before a miscreant President attempted to bring down Democracy and continues to spread his lies like manure.

We have moved into an era where power has become warped in meaning. No longer only about strength and possibilities, power now also means brute force misguided in a belief that it has God's permission to behave without impunity, and for some that it is all that matters in a world of changing priorities and great challenges. We are dangerously close to World War III.

Cluttered Present

Constantly living within reach of computer or cell phone, we may miss our chances to follow unexpected signs to fulfilling experiences beyond our control, bringing the world together in a neutral, experiential way, rather than through a comfortable connection to what is safe and known, leaving us with a false sense of control. We find ourselves living in a constant state of responding to what others deem important, neglecting rich opportunities of chance and surprise.

It's as though there is no longer an ability to make choices based on what is going on around one's immediate reality, but instead use an accumulation of choices that are pre-determined, programmed, accessed continuously. There is no way, in this view of reality, for the unknown, the 'serendipitous' moments to affect our lives. We are becoming a people who will inevitably lead the human experience to atrophy, as small clans and tribes shut themselves off from the open effect of otherness and change.

Young people have been trained to live in the future or an immediate connection to somewhere else. They have been led by technology and poor leadership (including coddling parenting and permissive psychology) to believe we can affect the future by feeding into it what we might like it to be, even if that future is based in unenlightened thinking. We cover up, change, largely marginalize the past because it is inconvenient. We have destroyed the power of the present, which is the only thing actually happening. Our present is so cluttered up with denial of the past and fear for the future that we fail to vote our best interests, crave to be led by autocratic politicians who appear to be more intelligent and capable than we believe we will ever be, and look aside when unable to process disturbing truths.

But it is an error in thinking to attempt to locate a time in human history to blame for our present. This stems from an inability to accept what is happening and address it from a present perspective. We believe if we can find where the beginning of the blame can be found we will understand how we came to this pass. Not so. Circumstances have been developing from the beginning of time. We can't explain, in terms of the past, a necessity to accept and deal with the present. It may help us to more deeply understand the problem, but fails when we attempt to effectively use it as an excuse to avoid dealing with what is presented now. Present context and all currently available facts of the immediate and continuing situation is often all we can rely on.

And then there is religion in the mix. So many millions of people believe the only purpose for their lives is to go on to a better after-life, so they kill themselves and others, or lie in order to remain in power and impose their beliefs on others long enough to be raptured up with the righteous few leaving the sinners to perish in their stink and slime.

3. HUMANITY

*Does interconnectedness
threaten a loss of personal freedom,
individual decision and sole commitment?*

Peace-Through-Grace

Money represents freedom, not power. The best use of money is peace-through-grace, an active use of resources to further recognize and honor the ease and benefits of all life – a kind of giving for hope, not gain.

The only time I ever had money, I invested in peace-through-grace, to sustain me for when I no longer had resources. Peace-through-grace is not the same as power. Power is having the strength to impose one's will upon others or to expand. Peace-through-grace is having the strength to encourage and help oneself and others to recognize and exercise their own will for the good of everyone concerned. In the short view, that would be the good of the partnership or the family, in the longer view that would be the good of the profession or the city, state, country, and in an even longer view that would be all of mankind on the planet, as well as all life, including that of the planet itself. Beyond the planet and other dimensions, peace-through-grace is a primary bridge because it is open and receptive, while eonomic power can be closed and opinionated, limiting more than it allows.

Faith

I remember a scientist being interviewed on the radio about how to discover 'faith' in the sciences. He said a really interesting way to think about things is that God had created a world where each thing was allowed to follow its own nature, evolve in ways which are free and not preordained by a 'divine architect'. Phenomena like an earthquake or tsunami can be explained by saying that the world God created even allows the undersea plates to follow their own tendencies. This is a really great argument against the rising tide of those who see the world as a grand plan created by a superior being. Nature is part of God, and to believe in a God who would create a world where free will gives rise to the shadow as well as the light, is to see the world as it is, and frees us from imposing some flawed interpretation of what the 'grand design' proposes.

In the last century there was a term called 'God's gaps' when science couldn't explain things. Conservative religious leaders pit science against faith, saying the more our world is explained by science, the further away from God we grow. Religious scientists believe that the more we know about our world through science, the closer to God we grow, because we are experiencing a deeper understanding of the changing nature of God by accepting the changing nature of our universe.

Is it possible to gather and unify the truly spiritual peoples of the world, who might penetrate religious establishments, begin to speak and practice their various religions without placing blame on those who do not believe as they do? I want to hear devout Muslims denounce forcibly the actions of suicide bombers. I want to hear Christians emphasize the Beatitudes which value the poor and have charity towards others without prejudice, rather than emphasizing the Ten Commandments which are the voice of a vengeful and strict ruler. Religions of all sorts have been used throughout the ages for purposes other than to create a world of peace, love and universal bounty, as interpretations of sacred texts have been bent to the will of human prejudice and used to subvert the purpose and application of most religion.

Has there always been more hate and disaster, war and lack of strong leadership than there are causes to rejoice in hope – of love and fortunate occurrence, of achievement and powerful examples of what is possible? Have we always been a world of hapless people, vulnerable to poverty and rife with loss of freedom? Our herd rules as a species, but remains blind to the ways to ease lives of pain.

Listening & Reading

Existentialism: a chiefly 20th Century philosophical movement embracing diverse doctrines but centering on individual existence in an unfathomable universe and the plight of the individual who must assume ultimate responsibility for his acts of free will without any certain knowledge of what is right or wrong or good or bad.

Stoicism: an ancient Greek school of philosophy teaching that virtue, the highest good, is based on knowledge; the wise live in harmony with Divine Reason (also identified with Fate and Providence) that governs nature, and are indifferent to the vicissitudes of fortune. The Stoics elaborate a detailed taxonomy of virtue – dividing virtue into four main types: wisdom, justice, courage, and moderation.

Radio interview about a son who claims he suffered from benign neglect, parented by loony giants.

A creative act is about putting something into the world that didn't exist before. If one merely mirrors the world there is very little creation involved.

When we move to the light, we open up darkness at the same time.

RadioLab program on Sleep: How our emotions rule our lives. Our brain registers emotional content in our daily lives more strongly than any other experience. Extremely intense content invades our dreams and haunts them, refuses to go away, so, when we don't get enough sleep, we lose the value of dreaming (a necessary cleaning process of each day's impact) and become increasingly ill; the long-range effect of severe trauma.

The reclaiming of the soul comes with the ability to see that God is in everything. To place blame, make war, divert attention from the truth – these have nothing to do with God.

Amazing sermon by Elder Bernice King, daughter of Martin Luther King Jr. and Coretta Scott King at Coretta's funeral, claiming that her ovarian cancer was symbolic of the problems of the world that are centered in the creative aspects of humanity. The vision of non-violence and need for a new birth was the crux of her plea, so powerful, especially coming from a daughter who just lost her mother.

Story also told at Coretta Scott King funeral: A little boy and his father were walking and discovered a large stone in the road. The little boy asked if his father thought he could move it. His father answered yes, if he used all the strength he had, so he pushed and struggled to move the stone and couldn't move it. Disappointed, he told his father he had been wrong, he couldn't move the stone, and his father replied "you didn't use all the strength you have, you didn't ask me to help you".

Thick Nhat Hahn, the Vietnamese Buddhist monk practices a walking meditation and advises his practitioners to "take the hand of a child, and walk in silence".

62. FLORA digital photo collage j.r–l.

VIII. FLIGHT

planning a future

Through A Wry Kaleidoscope is a first attempt at putting structure to a lifetime of journals. I began writing for my life in 1968. Seed material for this book was gleaned from journal entries between 2002 and 2009. On revisiting the material I was surprised to see, although the political arena was different in that post 9/11 world, it still presages our descent into political chaos and a world in thrall to authoritarian leaders. The original gleanings have been largely rewritten.

Editing these years of writing into a book gave me focus during the pandemic, transforming so many recorded past thoughts into a present whole. I continue to write daily. It has become my witnessing partner to an unlikely life, creating a humble artifact to bury in the cultural archeology of our time.

I write when I can't seem to focus or make sense of my day to day experience, working out problems in language, the stream of consciousness of an alien passing for normal in her attempt to process the struggle and contradictions of being a live and creative American woman born in 1943 and still here in 2022.

Much of this book is a recognition of the short-comings and troubles that cause humans to get in their own way. We take from the world what we can handle, if we know our limits.

Our unique sieve of processing information must remain actively alert to what doesn't move easily through. We nitpick our own facts, turning them to our advantage in a world where factions vie for reward and few manage to transpose information into something that furthers the way forward. So many choose to go backwards. So many resist change. So many are locked in limited function. This is a world we continue to navigate – a dark, fear-filled one where there is little truth and a surfeit of barriers, limits, blocks to momentum. Higher humanitarian intentions are few and far between, but they do exist and are to be celebrated when we find them.

I see our humanity as a shared gift, but also a shared process. We are all everyone and everyone is us. Now nearly into my 9th decade I continue to be amazed and challenged by what life presents.

Judith Ren-Lay
New York City
June 2022

63. TREE SAINT (hanging sculpture) j.r-l

Epilogue - APPRECIATION

Deepest thanks to those without whom this work might not exist...

Timothy Shepard – former student, valued friend whose unparalleled support saves me.

JoAnn Fragelette Jansen – who has been there for me always and helps in every way asked.

Kenneth Rinker – fellow artist who gave his artistic take on the writing as it evolved and left us too soon.

Jennifer Seidler – who read some of the original text and encouraged me to continue.

Stephanie Doba – a trusted reliable friend, who read early parts.

Jake Jacobson – who still believes in me after many years and offers support.

Cary Frumess – psychotherapist & trusted guide who always has the last word.

Emma Rose Brown – assistant extraordinaire.

Jim R. Moore – friend for many years, now publisher.

Diann Sichel and so many others who read early drafts and got back to me with comments.

... those who have been part of the weave of my life for decades: Andrea Star Reese, Ann Rower, Anne Iobst, Beo Morales, Beth Lapides, Bob Drake, Bob Holman, Brad Kessler, Buddy Hatcher, Carmen DeLavallade, Carol Mann, Cassie Mey, Chandler Romeo, Cheryl Sevier Johnson, Craig Tennis, David Cale, David Krueger, Davis Stewart, Debra Wanner, Diane Young, Dona Ann McAdams, Donald Byrd, Dudley Saunders, Ed Greer, Elizabeth Willoughby, Faye Dilgen, Frank Conversano, Gus Solomons jr, Hahn Rowe, Hank Smith, Jalalu-Kalvert Nelson, James Manfredi, Jane Friedman, Jean Brassard, Jenny Lynn McNutt, Jerry De La Cruz, Jill Gates, Jim Fouratt, Jo Shepard, Johanna Went, John Hagan, John Jesurun, John Kelly, Joshua Fried, Judson Duncan Hart, Julia Heyward, Juliet Myers, Justin Jones, Katherine Gallagher, Ken Butler, Kenneth King, Kevin Malony, Laurie Uprichard, Lisa Karrer, Lois Weaver, Lori E. Seid, Lucy Sexton, Margarita Gueguere, Marie Baker-Lee, Marion Appel, Mark Beard, Mark Fuller, Mark McCoin, Mark Russell, Michael Dorf, Michael Sharp, Mindy Levokove, Mio Morales, Molissa Fenley, Nancy Spanier, Nancy Zendora, Nicky Paraiso, Norman Frisch, Oana Botez, Pat Graf, Patrick Rawlins, Paula Court, Peggy Shaw, Randi Fain, Rebecca Moore, Reed Weimer, Renna Shesso, Ricardo Viviani, Rick Parker, Robert Coe, Rosanne Kadis, Ruis Woertendyke, Ruth Barnes, Sarah Connors, Sarah Schulman, Stephen Foreman, Stephen Petrilli, Steve Buscemi, Sue Lentz LeDuc, Sue Matsu, Suellen Epstein, Susanne Mueller, Suzette Martinez Theodorou, Antonia Tamara Kimberly Nathaniel, Traer & Emil Sunley, Valda Setterfield, Van Galligan, Vito Ricci, Wanda Phipps, William Neiderkorn, Yuko Otomo, Yolands Hawkins, Zo Curtis.

... the wisdom of those quoted or referred to: Native Americans, The I Ching, Sanjay Gupta, Emily Dickinson, Thick Nhat Hahn, The Desiderata, The Dalai Lama, Leo Tolstoy, Ben Kingsley, Bernice King.

... and for those friends and influencers who have sadly passed on: Blondell Cummings, Bob Auletta, Charles Ludlam, Chuck Shepard, Cynthia Novak, David Gordon, Diane Torr, Dorothy Madden, Dudley Williams, Ellen Stewart, Ernestine Stodelle, Ethyl Eichelberger, Frank Maya, Fred Holland, Georg Osterman, Gerry Doff, Helen Manfredi, Helen Russell, Howard Theiss, Jeff Buckley, Jo Andres, Joan Duddy, John Bernd, Kenneth Rinker, Linda Tarney, Mihally Theodorou, Nada Diachenko, Peter Moore, Peter Rose, Richard Bull, Robert Levithan, Ron Vawter, Spalding Gray, Steve Dalachinsky, Tarrant Smith, Tom Brazil, Tom Murrin, Viola Farber, William Harris ...... and my family ..... Dr. Earle Cleveland Haas, Myrtle Alexander Haas, Ted & Vera Haas, Carol & Dorothy Haas, Earlene Vilna Haas Lay, Willard Vernell Lay, Ren Lay, Harry & Cleda Lay, and Merlyn Lay Owens McKenzie.

IV. Bass

64. TRAGEDY *(24x14 ink on paper) j.r-l.*

Accidental Grit

when, in a violent instant,
a car hits you head-on

CONTENTS

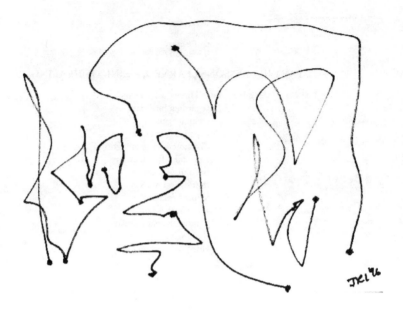

65.

INTRODUCTION

Physical pain can be the most intimate of experiences testing all aspects of the lives it touches. Challenges primarily of the body are often the toughest we can face, reducing our lives to a rare immediacy. As body and soul interact to clarify living, we are forced to come to terms with the magic lamp of body that contains the genie of our soul.

I was considered ill as a child. I still have report cards mentioning me as sickly. Not sure when I began to get healthy, but certainly it was sports and dancing and eventually cheerleading that led me to test the body. I have been 'testing' it all my life.

In my pre-art married days, physical education teaching and coaching sports kept me going. Periodically I would suffer from emotional overload and develop hives, migraine headaches or colitis, but, after a lot of suffering and problem solving I was able to conquer these stress-related diseases and keep moving on.

When I realized I was destined to be a dancer, I launched into training and eventual performing with discipline and inexhaustible energy. Then in 1989, at the age of 46, the heart exploded. I woke up with a blind spot in one eye and, upon further discovery, was diagnosed with a congenitally defective aortic valve. Instead of 3 cusps, I was born with 2. The result of this deformity, a lifelong accumulation of calcification finally started to throw pieces off the heart. I was told my heart was a time bomb and I might have a massive stroke at any time which could kill me, or leave me a vegetable. In light of this information, I agreed to undergo open heart surgery, the most scary and invasive test for my body to date. Fate stepped in to increase the difficulty leaving me with a staph infection, months in Bellevue Hospital trying to save the new valve, and then a second open heart surgery within the space of 3 months to replace the failing valve. I beat the odds in getting the infection AND in surviving the second surgery.

So I returned to the challenge of living as an artist with a mechanical heart valve and no money. I have never had money. I seem to just float along eking out an existence, assisted by a cheap rent-stabilized apartment left to me by a dear college friend. I would take odd jobs when they came up, and always put together enough residencies and grants and performing engagements or coaching gigs to make ends meet. From 1990 until 1995, after the heart surgeries, I produced an outpouring of original solo performance works involving design installation, dance, song and music created primarily from impulse and sheer determination.

But I had neglected to be vigilant as to the blood thinning medication I was required to take because of the metal valve. I suffered a minor knee injury while dancing and it exploded into a full blown compartment syndrome, requiring, once the problem was diagnosed, a fasciotomy, which is a cutting of the muscle sacs of the lower leg allowing the internal hemorrhage to drain. In many cases one may never walk normally after this injury. A year and a half later I was back in ballet class.

It was during this time I discovered the value of physical therapy. My injury was treated at the Harkness Center for Dance Injuries, a revered institution started by Marijeanne Liederbach. With the hands on brilliance of Faye Dilgen, Marshall Hagins, and Marc Hunter-Hall, I learned the essential lesson that if you do a little of just the right moves every day, amazing changes can occur.

I was always determined to ride this body as far as it would take me. I developed an intimate, intense conversation with it and attacked all new symptoms with the wisdom of my grandfather, a doctor who is the recognized inventor of Tampax. As a result of having Doc Haas in the family, we rarely went to any other doctors and home remedies were part of my upbringing. I seemed to always figure out what was going on by listening to my body and applying the cause and effect approach with remedies. Usually I hit on what would move the symptom through, rarely having to raise the alarm and seek further medical intervention.

A few years later, after creating a new solo involving the use of a large feather boa, I developed a cough that would not stop. Seeking medical advice led to every diagnosis logically available – Whooping Cough, Asthma, COPD, NTM, Pulmonary Hypertension – all arrived at due to my remaining in SoHo during and after the 9/11 attacks. I underwent copious tests and they had me on steroid inhalers for months. The only result was a case of shingles from the steroids. Eventually the cough went away. Upon reflection I suspect I was allergic to the feathers. Aggressive medical intervention often does harm. The body has its own sense of defense and timing. I have learned to allow it to fully participate.

In my late 60's I developed arthritis in my right hip and tried for years to treat it with physical therapy and aggressive Iyengar yoga, but it was looking like I was headed for a hip replacement when, out of the blue, a speeding cab hit me while crossing 6th Ave. fracturing both legs. Home remedies do not re-set bones or repair shattered ones.

During the immediate and ensuing years after being hit by a cab with the resultant desperate need to create a life without mobility, family, partner or close friend responsible for me, I taught myself how to communicate with a very specific email voice. When you are 'nobody's person' you have to carefully hone your contact skills in order to draw upon a community of acquaintances. I believe it is that email voice to which people responded enabling me to not only survive a very difficult time, but to learn and thrive. I worked on the emails as one would a very carefully crafted piece, re-working each one many times before sending it out.

So, except for a few introductory chapters, I tell this story from a constructed voice that came to my aid and carried me through. It was a lesson in a particular kind of writing, developed over time. It has always been my way, as a shape-shifting artist, to choose the form based on the content, the idea of what is being conveyed emotionally and intellectually. In this instance email was the primary way I could reach a large group of people and appeal to them for the necessary support system I required. And what was being written was the story of an inner life deeply challenged by circumstances. That is what this work offers and I believe it is best largely told in the original voice.

As I navigated the waters of difficulty, never imagining life as homebound and dependent, unable to practice my art which is so deeply conceived in body, it became clear to me, without family, partner or room-mate, reaching out to people I knew or who knew me was essential to moving through this time. In my 6 months of hospitalization following the accident, I gathered email addresses for those who expressed concern or who had been present and active as I pushed through the changes. After 5 years it became a list of 300, my 300 angels, each and every one of whom at one time or another contributed generous kind acts. I started to regularly write to them from my soul, a practice I created in order to save my inner life while dealing with a severely challenged vessel. Now 10 years on, *Accidental Grit* offers details of this life-changing accident, the aftermath, and my written attempts to convey a sense of it all.

Judith Ren-Lay
New York City
July 2021

PART I - NARRATIVE

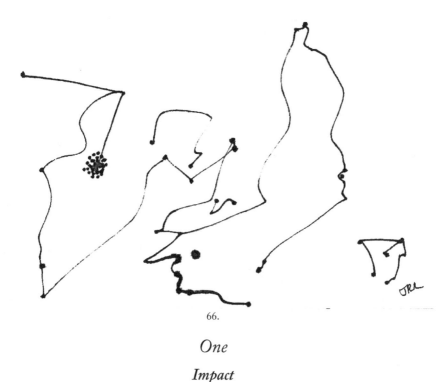

66.

One

Impact

A few days before my 68th birthday in January of 2011, I found myself sprawled on Sixth Avenue near Waverly Place aware my legs were seriously injured waving at passersby yelling "don't let him leave!" I had been crossing 6th Avenue with the light, when a speeding taxicab careened abruptly around the corner from Washington Place and plowed directly into me. I must have been facing the cab when it hit because I first fell forward over the hood and then backwards, my lower legs taking the full force of the collision. I remember realizing my glasses lay beside me. A lens had fallen out. Somehow I had the wherewithal to put the lens back in the frame, open my bag which was also beside me, and put the glasses back in their case before police and an ambulance descended on the scene.

The cab had stopped. I seem to recall there was a passenger. The driver had gotten out of the cab and the police were with him, a young dark man. I was being seen to by the EMTs. I could feel my left foot starting to swell and insisted they take the boot off before they had to cut it away. (In my mind I was thinking "These were, after all, relatively new winter boots").

I was still clearly lucid as the EMTs asked me for an emergency contact. That day I had gone out without phone or contact information, just my wallet and ID. Only two numbers came to mind – Gus Solomons, a close friend whose number I remembered, and Dennis Donohue, a man I had been (sort of) dating. The EMT who was with me in the ambulance let me use her phone to locate another number from the address of my nearest neighbors Yuko Otomo and Steve Dalachinsky. These four people contacted others and word spread.

I live alone. My parents and only sister passed on some years ago. I have always prided myself on an independent life, which was about to fundamentally change. Having created this life of dogged independence, I found myself suddenly in need of many people to help me through the biggest challenge of my life so far.

Two

The ER

Very soon Steve and Yuko managed to get into my apartment and retrieve my cell phone, so I was able to reach out for more help. By then I had arrived at Bellevue Hospital's Emergency Room and was being evaluated with x-rays and administered intravenous morphine for pain. I was no stranger to Bellevue, having spent 4 months there in 1990 for an aortic valve replacement and two open heart surgeries. Then again in 1995 I suffered a compartment syndrome and found myself at Bellevue again for six weeks to undergo a fasciotomy to my right lower leg without which they said I might actually have lost the leg. These were both sudden, traumatic events and each took years of recovery. The ins and outs of emergency care were not new to me. I've learned the hard way-sometimes one must be a bit of a nuisance to have needs met in a hospital setting. I call it negative assertiveness. 'Ask nicely up to 3 times and then freak out' was a practiced coping mechanism.

Word came from the tests – I had a fractured tibial plateau on the right side and a shattered talus on the left. I was destined for three months total non-weight-bearing, meaning without walking or using my legs for anything at all, and then, for many more months, only with assistance. I had no idea at the time the rehab facility care would stretch to 6 months, one of the reconstructions would fail from lack of blood supply, and I would spend five years homebound in nearly constant pain.

Because of my artificial heart valve I take coumadin, a blood thinner. Reconstructive surgeries had to be delayed until the coumadin in my system was entirely absent to prevent bleeding out. So I was wheeled into a room on the wards and celebrated my 68th birthday there, with many concerned visitors bringing beautiful flower arrangements and an outpouring of good will. All was witnessed by me in a bit of shock, a fog of morphine and general sense of disbelief. I joked that Fate's secretary had simply made a clerical error. This accident was supposed to be for someone named Len-Ray. It really wasn't my turn after what I had already been through.

Three

Morphine Daze

And so it began. Insensitive nurses, hospital noises through the night, dozens of Residents peering over the notes of the Attending Physicians. Wheeling me out and in for X-rays, blood tests, administering drugs for pain, for sleep, for anxiety. Psych consults and pain management consults and internists and cardiologists and radiologists and the surgeons and their teams, and the constantly changing nurses who now were my sole keepers in most ways. I could feed myself, but was not allowed to get up for any reason, so I soon learned the joys of the bedpan. In addition to bringing down my coumadin levels those first two weeks, the opiates were causing crushing constipation requiring the indignities of what they call an *extraction*. I think you get the picture.

One attempt to reposition the shattered ankle bone because they thought it might give the surgeon a 'better result' ended in a level of pain I had never experienced. He gave me an injection in the foot, told me it would block the pain and then proceeded to 'yank' the foot into place. I nearly blacked out before I began howling and they then wheeled me down to x-ray where I had to wait on the gurney until they could take me, yowling uncontrollably all the way there and during and back to the room. This was not negative assertiveness, this was enduring a torture far beyond anything before or since. I was inconsolable and an embarrassing herald to all hospital staff. That was the first time they put a guard on the door. Of course anybody must be crazy if they allow themselves to display the full expression of their response to painful treatment. I soon became the poster child for lack of repression. I reacted honestly to everything, especially when it hurt. This was the beginning of saving the mind trapped in the injured body.

Familiar Surroundings

I was trained at an early age to equate sugar with love. My mother would bake brownies or make fudge when an emotional bit of tension occurred in the family, rather than addressing it in any way. I soon realized this as a glimmer of universal truth. Sugar swamps everything. People want to shower us with delicious treats, not knowing what else to do. Not only three different kinds of birthday cake arrived those first ten days, but while I was in hospital, before I was even transferred to rehab, there were cookies, chocolate bars, cannolis, all sorts of chips, flan, chocolate covered walnuts and almonds, even an ice cream bar. When all else fails, give sugar! I was raised by this premise even though my grandfather was a doctor. As time wore on I began to experience the heartbreak that must come with obesity through inactivity and deliciously bad food.

Surgery was scheduled; I was informed they were going to repair both injuries at once – one team on the right tibial plateau and another on the shattered talus. Post-surgical x-rays show prominent pieces of metal pins and braces creating scaffolding for the broken parts of bone to heal. I've been under for surgery twice before, so I was relieved they at least would put me out this time, so pain wouldn't hit until later. At this point I had full belief they would fix me and put my trust in the Attending Physician – Dr. Toni

Mclauren. She was known by my long-time physical therapy guru Faye Dilgen and had offices at the Hospital for Joint Diseases where the Harkness Center for Dance Injuries was also located at the time. A bit of anything familiar in this circumstance is extremely helpful, and relying on wise friends who may help navigate strange, turbulent waters is essential.

My lawyer friend of sixteen years, Michael Sharp, was at my bedside the second day to take charge of all legal issues. I was so relieved to rely on his expertise in these matters, I paid little attention to what I later found out was a serious gap in the justice system when it comes to traffic injuries. The No Fault laws in New York State award 'anybody' injured by an automobile a basic $50,000 for medical expenses and that's it. No driver is charged, nobody to sue, no other recourse. Long gone are the days when, if hit by a cab you could sue for hundreds of thousands. This is a form of tort reform favoring the cab companies. I believe the driver who hit me was out driving the next day endangering the lives of others.

Four

Transfer to Rehab

These days they move you out of hospital as soon as possible. I was in Bellevue from Jan 5th (when I was ambulanced to the Emergency Room post-accident) until January 22nd – just over two weeks. The first surgeries were performed January 10th and on January 22nd I was handed a list of sub-acute (Rehab) facilities from which to choose and went with Village Care on Houston Street, a relatively new one at the time. Since then it has become the go-to place for many friends and associates sustaining injury or undergoing surgery. I chose it because it was downtown and closest to my apartment. And so began six months of living in rehab.

My first room was shared and cramped. Any ability to cope was becoming extremely frayed. Between the constant pain, bad food, testy nurses and rude administrators, I 'lost it' repeatedly. Their solution was to move me to a private room. Negative assertiveness in action.

171

My paper agenda of the time confines itself to names of visitors, arrival of gifts and flowers, food and calls. Since my sanity depended entirely on the kindness of friends, these were the most significant things to me during this time. People kept me in flowers and plants adorning the big window looking out over Film Forum across from Village Care on Houston Street - my non-ambulatory garden of gifted delights.

The first post-operative appointment with the surgeon was not until March 10th. At that point I had been totally non-weight-bearing on both legs for two months, sleeping on my back with both legs elevated. I would not be able to try to stand until April 8th. I stood for 45 seconds.

There were repeated attempts to force me to leave. Although my insurance covered everything, they played all sorts of games to maximize their profit and take advantage of anyone who is in a precarious situation. Without a specific person designated as my emergency contact, I was in a constant state of defending myself. Repeated mistakes were made having to do with care – most alarmingly trying to give me the wrong medicine numerous times. If I hadn't been completely on top of my own care I could have easily come out of there permanently impaired. As it was, staying alert and making demands was partly what kept me going.

It was the 12th of April before I was able to shift from wheelchair to toilet – having spent three months on a bed-pan.

Physical Therapy

The physical therapy was experienced as gross and over-loading. Their objective was to push as hard as they could, but my body has its own pace. I went to physical therapy in hospital gowns until JoAnn Jansen sent me snap-on pants into which I could roll, both legs being in casting boots. I suspect they viewed me as resistant, but I was anything but. I was anxious to absorb and integrate the changes. I did a lot of my own exercises in my room and performed intensive self-massage daily when I could bear it. Ice was my constant companion.

As I began to recover, pain became a huge impediment to recovery with beginning weight bearing, carrying around a heavy cumbersome boot, and asking the legs to hold me up with a lot of the work in the arms. Excruciating pain followed me into the room, throughout the night and into the morning.

Supplies From Home

By this time I had been able to retrieve very little from home, having arrived with only the clothes I had been wearing. It was easier for folks to bring things to me obtained from outside than to try to find them in my apartment. I did not know it at the time, but I wouldn't even have access to my computer until February 13th when Marion Appel and Margarita Guergue accomplished the awesome task of attending to a list of what I required from home. They took on a Herculean task for someone who is used to doing everything on her own. This was the beginning of wrestling with a growing dependency.

Journal Entries January & February 2011

- Life here is colorful and descriptive of the lost, downtrodden, weary and extremely ill.

- Cloaked in acceptance.

- Scars – a visible journey of the body's mishaps.

- I ask for a pain management consult but nobody is available, so I cry and bear it, as hope leaks out with every awkward step. I kept asking myself "how can I possibly live like this"? My once available good nature and grace under fire have been replaced by an ugly demeanor due to too much pain medication and institutional foul ups. Some evil twin now inhabits this damaged body struggling to walk again.

PART II - DEAR FRIENDS

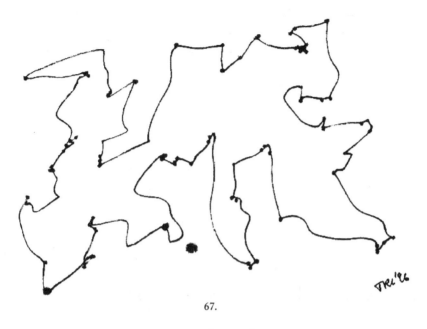

67.

2011 - Year One

March 22
not yet walkin'

Just an update to those who have contacted me in the aftermath
of having been hit by that cab on Jan 5, 2011.

Driver literally struck the legs out from under me.
Bad fractures to left ankle and right tibia at the knee.
Reconstructive surgeries Jan 10.
Mar 10 xrays show plates and pins holding bones together,
but still not strong enough to bear weight.

Life in bed is not what those of you working too hard might imagine!

Mostly huge hugs and thanks for those who have called, sent care
packages, flowers and plants, cards with well wishes and Facebook
notes.

Special shout out to those who have come to visit, kept me going with supplies, retrieved things from home, accompanied me to clinic appointments, stopped by to bring food and helped out with so many things I can't do myself.

This is going to be a long slog, learning to walk on newly constructed limbs, so I will continue to need this blessed army of those willing to help out for some months yet to come.

March 31
visiting

Thanks to all who have taken time to visit and send things during these nearly three months since I was taken out by that cab. Contact with friends grounds me in the fight, and since most of you are wildly busy, it takes a large pool of generous souls to keep the human element alive.

I'm a captive ear and able to listen. Still unable to stand or walk, but the mind seems relatively intact.

I am overwhelmed by the continued generosity of so many and find myself curiously re-examining dogged independence as a lifestyle.

April 8
healing update

Saw the surgeon yesterday and my crazily reconstructed tibia and talus have been determined healed. X-rays of the reconstructions are scary awesome. More metal than bone in both locations. I now have permission to bear weight, but can only begin to do it with the physical therapist present, so am once again into the unknown. Another six weeks and I see the Dr. again. I'm afraid this is going to be the painful time, getting circulation, breathing and muscles functioning again after so long. I have NO calf muscles whatsoever!

Returning home will depend entirely on my walking status, so I continue this stressful institutional life. There is some much needed fund-raising in the works, and the beginnings of organizing a group I'm calling Operation Apartment Rescue to prepare the way.

I can't begin to thank you for all the visits, calls, plants and flowers, goodies, cards and care packages, meals, errands and help with everything I can't do for myself. Keep 'em coming!

But most of all I appreciate the human contact and discovering there so many good people who care.

April 15
pushing through

Another week into this long process of post trauma and there are changes. I have permission to bear weight, but no one told me how difficult it would be. I can only barely stand supported by my arms on a walker for around a minute at a time. Can't feel the floor, no balance. Still haven't taken that first step. Enormous pain requires more narcotics and resultant digestive upset.

Good news is, with the help of David and Tim, I have re-arranged the furniture here at Village Care and can now access the entire room in a wheelchair, able to water the plants, retrieve things from low shelves and even make it to the bathroom on my own.

Human contact with so many of you has made this fight possible. I send grateful love to all, especially those who continually take time out of their busy schedules to call and visit, send care packages, shop for supplies, retrieve things from the apartment, and take care of all the things I can't do for myself all these many months since the accident.

In this new phase I am struggling with a loss of hope and confidence. Flowers and plants seem to bring the most cheer, as the 'garden' reminds me life is in process and beautiful aspects will eventually emerge from this struggle.

April 25
resurrection pending

Phase 1 – Bellevue where many of you rushed to my aid just after the cab accident.
Phase 2 – transfer to Village Care Rehab and the seemingly endless 3 months wait for the bones to heal while I lay like a mummy casted and braced, unable to bear weight on either leg and where so many of you came through to provide me with the essentials of food, supplies and human support.
Phase 3 – bone reconstructions having healed, began what is supposed to be a 6 week course of weight bearing physical therapy

learning to walk again.
Into the 3rd week of Phase 3. Surprising amount of pain in the process. Still determined to keep you informed and in the loop.

Beginning to think about what it will mean to return to my apartment and how much needs to be done to prepare the way indicating a continuing need for the assistance of friends.

So far it's been a brilliant effort of 'sharing the burden' considering everyone on this list is either miles away and/or extremely busy. Thanks, thanks, thanks and again thanks for all you do.

What I am learning about survival under stress:
  – adapt without surrender
  – be tolerant, but clearly communicate essential boundaries
  – expect little and express much gratitude for what comes

May 6
early walking

Well, I've been 'patient' for going on eighteen weeks (or four and a half months). That even beats my Bellevue stay of '89-'90!

Yesterday I walked again, after a fashion. Extremely slow and painful, with a walker. These do not feel like my legs, and muscles long fallen into disuse ache into the night.

Of course I am grateful for every step and put effort towards all angles on the healing process, but I am also exhausted. Just trying to stay focused and proactive is a creative challenge under these circumstances. Village Care, the rehab facility where I have spent all but the first two weeks of this endurance test, looks new and fancy on the outside, but the inner workings are a nightmare. Too few workers to adequately cover patient care, confusion about insurance with threats of early dismissal handled rudely by social workers who really should consider another career choice, endless delays when asking to see a doctor or to have emergency tests, repeated attempts to administer the wrong drugs. I have to be constantly alert and act as my own advocate at all times.

But the extra food drawer is stocked full of goodies, the plants and flowers thrive, supplies are often brought just when needed, and the human conversations about all our lives are a source of constant strength.

As little as I can project, I suspect I will be here several more weeks. David and Stephen are beginning to prepare the way in my apartment, and Tracey is working on a plan for my care after returning home.

Fundraising project, begun just after the accident, was stalled. Hoping it can start up again. Deep gratitude to a few spontaneous early donations keeping my head above it.

Once again thanks for all you do. If you no longer want to receive these updates, just let me know and I will take you off the list. On the other hand, if you know someone who may not know of my situation and should be included, let me know that, too.

Yours in faith and healing,

May 14
every day, in every way …

When I started these weekly updates I just wanted to keep in contact with what has proven to be an essential group of individuals who have contributed massively to my healing process. I now realize it is an ongoing chronicle of this unbelievable time of trauma, response, and rallying forces in order to stand up to some strange and twisted dealings of fate.

On the one hand, I am indeed taking walks with two physical therapists in tow, relying entirely on a walker. I told them yesterday it must feel like walking the dog.

On the other hand it is extremely painful, I do not feel the front part of the left foot on the ground, and afterwards my feet swell up so much I have to encase them in ice for 30 minutes, massage them deeply for another 20 minutes each, and remain exhausted the rest of the evening.

On the one hand, I have nearly everything I need except for things from my apartment which, strangely enough, seem the toughest to get. So many treasured trips to drugstores and Trader Joe's and Whole Foods for supplemental food and supplies of everything from Epsom salts to black pepper to castor oil and saran wrap!
On the other hand, I didn't have a visitor all week until Debra and

Joan brought some requested supplies. I realize it isn't the supplies as much as the visits that give me strength, but often it's the asking for supplies that prompts a visit.

The garden has suffered as far as fresh flowers are concerned, but I dried bunches of roses, and now dried arrangements make the window seem alive, long after the bloom of color. This living, dying process has been a great source of pleasure and hope.

I have recently re-read all the lovely cards and letters that have arrived over these many months and am amazed so many of you have taken time out of your busy lives to think of me and send healing wishes and gifts. A thousand thank yous.

The future reveals itself slowly, pretty much day to day. Village Care has stopped making noises about premature discharge and physical therapists are not pushing too fast, too hard as before. I spend the days and evenings in healing practices, grateful for this grace period before I am strong enough to return to my apartment, which may be in as little as two weeks, but more likely early June.

May 29
upcoming home-coming

Increased healing brings increased uncertainty.

My doctor recommends two more weeks at Village Care Rehab where I have been recovering since January. Date certain for going home can't be confirmed until after Memorial Day, when the social workers are available to set up a discharge plan. This week the apartment is being cleaned, and necessary adaptations to shower and studio sleeping completed. All praise to David Krueger and Stephen Petrilli for their Herculean efforts to prepare the way.

Quite frankly, I am terrified to be on my own again. Although it feels like a huge relief, it is only the beginning of another phase of recovery, and I will continue to need a lot of friends to keep humanity and supplies rolling.

It is unknown just how much ambulatory facility I will have upon discharge, but we are hoping I will be able to use two canes to climb the 18 stairs to my apartment. Daily I grow stronger, now walking with a walker, but will continue to need physical therapy for many months, initially in-home and then as an out-patient.

Even though I crave the solace of my little SoHo cave of an apartment surrounded by my own things, it will be hard to leave the dubious luxury of being incarcerated in a rehab center with basic needs met.

Laughter has been one essential partner during this time. Not surprisingly, a new kind of laugh – laughing through my teeth – has been added to the repertoire.

I remain in awe of the spontaneous outpouring of help and well wishes from so many who have been a real lifeline to this point.

Miraculously there is a Benefit/Home-coming party for me at City Winery 155 Varick St on Tuesday, June 14th from 6:30-9pm, through the good graces and concern of Michael Dorf and Ed Greer from Knitting Factory days. A surprise blessing.

June 6
five months later

Sending this to all who have expressed an interest in my situation, including Facebook folks who have commented on my page. Just let me know if you want off the list.

an update and re-consideration of the phases of this moon-beam:

Phase 1 – hit by a cab Jan 5th. Reconstructive surgeries to left talas bone and right tibial plateau on Jan 10th. Two weeks at Bellevue.

Phase 2 – transferred to Village Care Rehab on West Houston Street Jan 22. Endured 3 months of non-weight bearing status (meaning no weigh at all on either leg). Pretty much on my back with legs elevated the entire time, enduring the indignities of bed-pans and the constant mishandling of drugs and care.

Phase 3 – April 8th given permission to bear weight by the surgeon and began to remember how to stand and eventually walk with increased pain and psychic challenges.

Phase 4 – after eight weeks of weight-bearing physical therapy I will be discharged from Village Care Rehab on Saturday, June 11th. I am walking slowly requiring enormous concentration with the assist of two canes. Continued recovery at home for many more months.

I could never have gotten through (with a relatively sound mind) if it had not been for a huge group of people lending their energy and well wishes. I have managed because of the many care packages from afar and regular visits bearing gifts from those closer to home. So many people have given so much.

1) Parts of us die every day and we notice it most when we lose health, livelihood, friends.

2) The acceptance and tolerance of even the worst luck or the most offensive behavior is a cultivatable skill.

3) My circle of friends has been completely reshuffled. This will continue until all of us are dead and gone.

June 12
long walk home

On my last days at Rehab, people see me walking and say "so beautiful". Stephanie cries, having been there from the first. I say "it's all smoke and mirrors, baby", since these do not feel like my legs but someone else's, someone very like a newborn colt, trying to stand and take those first tentative steps. My left foot is still numb from toe to instep so I don't feel where I am on the foot. My right knee can't hold much stress. But I take to heart my priceless Alexander lessons with Diann Sichel and attempt to relax and allow, float and lift, apparently creating an illusion.

I have learned how to:
- draw strength from people, hopefully without burdening them.
- ask in order to discover what is possible.
- accept what comes and be grateful.
- say no when the answer is clear.
- accept the limitations of self and others.
- plead "unacceptable" when incompetence threatens well-being.
- bear the greatest of pain with laughter.
- appreciate the simplest pleasures in life – a shower, tasty food, excessive kindness given freely, the beauty of flowers.
- put my own situation in a perspective to encompass an understanding of all our situations.
- manage with the bare minimum and gradually get most needs met.
- focus on basic tasks and find it leads to deeper thoughts.
- value people for who they are, what they bring to my life, and what

I bring to theirs.

I am home now, facing the re-orientation to solo living and hoping you, part of this courageous group who have facilitated my recovery, will not become distant. I embrace a growing need to share my life, such as it is.

June 17
the benefit

With the help of a stunning advisory panel, I managed to get into clothes and make-up and attend the wonderful benefit arranged by the awesome Michael Dorf and Ed Greer at the City Winery Tuesday night June 14th. Overwhelmed by so many people turning out, I entered, teetering on my two canes, with fear and trepidation, but Ed had arranged for me to be seated in a safe place and my stalwart girlfriends stayed by my side all night long.

Hank Smith did an amazing tap dance, the epitome of cool, and Hahn Rowe managed to capture my entire experience in his musical offering. I cried. Ed Greer, the master mind of the entire event then humorously and effectively auctioned off several items. Much great wine was consumed by all including many bottles of the celebratory wine of the evening, the Ren-Lay Reserve.

I was often overwhelmed and delighted to see so many wonderful people coming out on my behalf. Beginning to wonder if saying thank you too much, dilutes its meaning, but I seem to have spent 5 months and counting saying just that – over and over and over again.

In love and growing gratitude,

June 25
home is where the work is

I am experiencing some kind of rebirth, requiring 5 months of gestation in a fetal position flat on my back with legs raised higher than my heart. I must return to that position for much of each day cutting into efforts to get back to work, work being a disabled attempt to reclaim the sanity of my apartment of 40 years, abandoned so long and in massive disarray. Coming home felt more like coming to a cluttered, filthy hell where the Xmas decorations were still up. It took 5 people 7 hours just to clear enough space for me to be able to sleep here that first day home. Thank God for Patricia who drove, and to Stephen, Tracey, Stephanie, Debra and Diann who witnessed the disaster area and helped to make space, and to Cassie and David who came the next day.

While I slowly pour through a lifetime of accumulated belongings, I imagine I have died and am my own daughter, sadly losing things of the past, setting up for an unknown future.

I'm made rudely aware of how life seems filled with trivial impediments to progress. The buzzer to the front door is broken and I can't let people in unless we tape the door open. Over a week home and it's still not fixed. Then the 20 year old tv set is giving me a picture with red on the left side of the screen and green on the right. Today the vacuum cleaner cord refuses to pull out of its winder and lock, so it just keeps rewinding back into the machine. Light bulbs go out, dust is in every corner, on every object I touch.

There seems to be nothing but work in order to uncover an environment where I can re-address the healing. But I am glad to be working and especially glad for the friends who come daily, observing my progress, assisting the effort, and lending support in so many ways. These updating emails are my way of embracing you all, as part of the ongoing process of recovery.

July 13
no sliding home

This list has grown to over 200, all from concerned folks learning of my plight and responding with massive generosity, kindness and concern. Tons of return acknowledgements and donation receipts remain long overdue. I beg patience.

Visit to surgeon last week confirmed the ankle fracture is not healing as she had hoped, so I am facing another 6 weeks of virtual homebound life. I sent a plea to those nearby who might be available to visit, as I have a new sense of the value of people in my life. Periodic interruptions having to do with the lives of others brings meaning to times of solitude.

These first weeks home have been consumed with tasks of re-invention. As I witness the accumulations of nearly 40 years of NYC life, I find myself re-weaving everything I touch into some kind of future, a future of unknowns. I've eliminated half my clothes, tons of files and many collected letters from a lifetime. I found the studio in extreme disarray after five months of neglect and now look at everything very differently.

Lose things of the past, simplify with fewer choices in all categories of supplies, re-think the value of everything owned, saved, stored. I sense we often live amid our accumulated objects, but it doesn't seem to me to be the strongest way to live.

This process of re-weaving requires ripping apart and, although good for my mind, takes a toll on my injuries. Intensive healing practices are set aside in favor of creating a space within which to truly heal in all ways. Chaos and clutter are not my friends. Extreme focus is required.

July 18
grey dragons

Well, it was bound to happen. Just a month home, having re-organized the next healing cocoon, and dark dragons are swooping around, blowing smoke. It's becoming increasingly difficult to accept the situation, see clearly, move through available choices.

Loyal, regularly present friends take time out of active lives and speak to me of the future. I can't see more than a day or so ahead. Of more concern, I avoid addressing my body, painfully aware of the obstacles. After 40 years of taking all my cues from it, this body now resists. I begin to wonder if I will ever regain my physical center, ever walk free of pain, ever manage to be in charge of life once again, ever be capable of moving about the city alone, shopping, attending events, going out to be the visitor instead of the visited. The last person I heard got hit by a cab in New York City became a nun.

I try to remind myself my wonderful supporters are counting on me and send and bring tons of strength and energy, but after six months of struggling for equilibrium at every phase of this tangled twist of fate, I am weakening.

These moments of written reflection (my Accidental Blog) often carry some uncomfortable truth. As with matters largely at the mercy of the mind, this too, shall pass. Still yours with hope in healing,

August 2
time tells

Nearly seven months on and I sense a need to redefine normal.
Changes occur in the foot as feeling returns, leading to more pain.
How many people understand what it is like to live in constant pain?
More than we think, and likely some of you. I become more and
more aware of the challenges we all are facing and mine just one
voice in the cacophony.

The more time I spend with friends, the more meaning gets squeezed
from shared facts and trials of living – time, of course, being the
greatest of gifts to share.

My recovery has been blessed with inspiring stories from other
people's lives. A myriad of family crises and celebrations, sibling
rivalries, the challenges of parental aging and troublesome grown
children, the magical behavior of young children, stresses of work
environments, response to health challenges, births and deaths –
these proofs of life, when shared, bring us more closely together
invigorated with future hope.

Thanks to the wonderful City Winery Benefit and generous
donations, I have the means to keep my basic needs met for a few
months to come. Re-entry into the outside world, however, is
developing very slowly. Last time I went out on my own I was hit by
a cab ... more than physical recovery is required.

There is at last a relative calm in the studio except for the fact it is
also bedroom, gym, entertainment center, recovery room. I imagine
how to create a normal bed out of the space which now contains a
deserted loft bed accessible only by climbing up the furniture. (It
seems clear to me I am not going to do that again any time soon). I
stumble into the kitchen intending to eat, and end up eating whatever
requires the least preparation. Friends stop over and feed me.

I grumble a bit – then count my blessings.

August 11
not ready for prime time
Besides the obvious cries for help, these emails have:
  – helped clear my mind and put an extreme experience into

perspective

    – enabled me to gather and embrace the willing, the concerned, the appreciative

    – provided a way to give thanks for the myriad kindnesses that have come my way consistently from so many, over such a long period of time

I would love to report all is progressing well and life after injury is beginning to take shape. Unfortunately I cannot say that. As of this Friday, my nine weeks of 'grace' with a home care program will abruptly come to an end and I will be largely on my own for the first time since January when this endurance challenge began. A few friends are making themselves available regularly and make all the difference.

Also have a few tricks for extended mobility – rolling desk chairs in studio & kitchen, a rolling stool enabling me to function reasonably well in the kitchen, and, of course, my trusty two canes when wheeling is not possible. I can manage the stairs, walk short distances without carrying anything, but incredibly slowly, with tremendous insecurity.

I'm yearning for balance – between pain and medication, between rest and work, between taking care of myself and needing things done I simply cannot do. It's tough on my pride to admit such infirmity, to present myself as so much less than I remember. In addition to the occasional emotional outbursts and dire physical break-down, I am now battling an agoraphobic resistance to being in the world.

In spite of all, the mind still remembers clarity. It comes, from time to time. Ever your grateful fellow traveler on this strange journey that is life.

August 22
mindful of milestones

All praise email. The sheer volume of communications these past months of confinement and detachment overwhelms me, as I see how this event has personalized my ability to reach others and offer a true self to lives of mutual interest.

The words I share are coming from a different place now. Instead of simply emptying my mind and forming thoughts into language, I am thinking about what you might like to hear about my situation that could perhaps serve to illuminate all our lives.

For instance, I am concentrated and mindful of every action I take, including how I sit on the new rolling kitchen stool. If I just plop down unconsciously it will quickly roll out from under me. I move through daily tasks slowly and methodically to avoid a fall, while taking full advantage of the mobility aids of wheels and sticks for support.

Weekly milestone – I visited my surgeon last week by myself. Tiring (took a 2 hour nap upon returning home) but liberating! Walking short distances incredibly slowly and with enormous effort on two black and silver canes in my Hi Top PF flyers, the only shoe that seems to help.

Doctor says right tibia healed – pain from the metal plate near the surface irritating the tendons as it begins to move more. Left talus "not filled in" and "may have collapsed a bit" so it is a different shape now but has improved with the 20 minutes a day home ultrasound machine.

Your visits and contacts continue to feed me in so many ways. Keep 'em coming.

August 31
humbling storms

Post-Irene: What a good weekend to be a shut-in! Thanks for all the concerned calls and emails. Hope you and yours emerged unscathed. I rode out Irene quite dry and safe in my protected cave in SoHo with plenty of food and emergency supplies of flashlights, candles and water at the ready, watching the blanket of news coverage on every channel. It was a massive storm. "Once again, the weather has everybody talking ..." Earth, fire and water exhibit powers capable of decimating life on the planet. We are humbled.

September 10
exertion vs. adaptation
The water in my building runs scalding to ice cold except around 2am when most residents are asleep, so I stay up late when I want to take

a shower. Makes me think about how much we adapt to things as we find them vs how much we exert the effort it takes to accomplish major changes. In the case of a calming shower, adaptation seems the wisest choice.

I refuse, however, to fully adapt to an invalid life. Change is happening, however slowly. I do what I can to keep moving without upsetting the day to day acceptance that has gotten me this far. I avoid pushing, fully enjoy my computer, books and movies, eat way too many sweet treats, and welcome blessed visitors bearing distraction, caring and gifts. I don't often fret over what 'isn't' yet working. Instead I remember to celebrate what 'is' and nudge everything else along as gracefully as possible.

Monday, the 12th, after our 9/11 ten-year anniversary, and after two weekends consumed by Hurricane Irene and the end of yet another season of life as a shut-in, I have an appointment to begin outpatient physical therapy. Limited by Medicare, I chose a facility close by, traveling being my biggest challenge. I am dreading what I know will be an increase in pain, but realize it's time. I'm scripted for 2-3 times a week for 12 weeks. Life in the world, on a schedule, begins.

Hoping the fall season will occasion some 'walk-abouts' with you as the weather cools and invites.

September 25
dip and rally

Sorry for the long missive, but ....

Last Friday was to be my 4th work session with the new physical therapist. It was a day of torrential rains in New York. I put on the PF flyers and a raincoat, but when it came time to head out and hail a taxi, I broke down and couldn't do it. Ended up calling Carlo deCastro, the PT, and canceling. Then completely fell apart. Crying and howling uncontrollably for a long time.

Calls are in to my trusted psychotherapist.

This miraculous juggling act is getting harder with time, not easier, accompanied by a dropping off of regular visitors. My spirit lapses as I ride along through dips and rallies and begin to wonder if I will ever walk easily again without pain. We never think just being able to walk

189

is a blessing, we just take it for granted. The stronger I seem, the more I am challenged. Each dip seems to be followed by a rally, but there is a lurking fear of the dip that fails to rally.

I never imagined I would have to delay or arrange to have done by someone else, over such a long period of time, virtually everything needed to keep the functional part of life ongoing – cleaning the apartment, doing the laundry, making sure there are regular meals, mail in and out, getting supplies, trash & recycle gathering and dumping, bank deposits, visits to the optometrist, the dentist, not to mention all social activities in the world requiring being mobile. When you can't do the simple things, life presents insurmountable stresses. Breathless and weepy trying to take care of myself alone, mealtimes come and, rather than struggle with the simple tasks of preparation & cleaning up, I order in and spend money I really shouldn't be spending.

I do remember to be thankful I am able to shower, dress, and otherwise tend to personal care and manage to pay my bills, thanks to many generous donations – but each day presents a new challenge and, nine months in, I'm getting tired.

These email updates become my connection to the world. That you continue to receive them is saving my life. I wish the messages were consistently upbeat, but if you can't handle the truth you probably wouldn't be on this list.

October 2
putting humpty dumpty back together

What a ride!

All acts of overcoming the odds are preceded by "in spite of..." indicating spite is being focused on the offending impediment. My ankle doesn't like spite. It calms down with rest and light exercise and absolutely won't hold me up without incredible pain when I push. Since beginning outpatient physical therapy I am much worse. I am scheduled to return to the surgeon Thursday for a CT Scan because they can't seem to figure out why I am still, after all this time, in so much pain.

The apartment reconstruction to lower my loft bed begins Tuesday so a stalwart group of the able-bodied have been helping me scrunch everything into the nooks and crannies of the rest of the apartment in order to empty the loft room and allow for work to be done. Mark, who is doing the work, says he doesn't like to work in a stressful environment. No pressure there!

Yesterday Oana slow walked me to a Sleepy's 4 blocks away to pick out a mattress. Diann met us. There was only one model within the parameters of my research and it cost more than I had hoped. In order to try it out, since the store had no elevator, I had to climb down and then up again a set of stairs about the same as the ones to get in and out of my apartment. Barely made it home after Diann threatened to carry me!

By Wednesday evening, when the mattress is being delivered, I will be ready to reverse the process and begin to put everything back together again. I will need all the help I can get.

My shrink says I have to be as squeaky a wheel as is necessary to get the assistance I still so desperately need.

Such is the way things are going. I still try to laugh but frequently cry at the absurdity of it all.

October 12
complications in healing

Just a quick factual update to all those who have been concerned and so generous over these many months since I was hit by that cab in early January.

CT Scan shows talus not healing as Dr. had hoped. It is not shaped right, has collapsed a little and still not filled in. The source of increased pain is something called post traumatic arthritis in the sub talar joint (there is no cartilage left between the two large foot bones,) something that sometimes happens after such a devastating trauma to the foot. Invasive solution suggested is another surgery to fuse the talus and calcaneus, requiring another three months non-weight-bearing on the foot. The fusion of those bones would limit range of motion, but might eliminate the constant pain inhibiting my ability to walk. I am really distraught – possibly facing another surgery requiring another three months of non-weight-bearing. In addition, the large toe joint on that foot is fused/locked. It is called hallux rigidus, a condition also requiring surgery. Seems I'm not getting through this so smoothly as all had hoped. Thought you would appreciate medical details, even though it's not all that is going on.

I battle growing demons and, sorry to report, have lost a dose of the inspiring grace so many of you have credited me with during this long ordeal.

With love and faith in the power of friendship,

October 19
wheezing and a cough

Little glimpses of clarity come as I contemplate what is going on and how to make the best choices. Considerations on further foot surgery have not been completely resolved, but rather than rushing to do it, I'm gathering information and taking my time.

Contracted a bout of bronchitis (surprise, surprise!) Days of constant coughing, making an inhuman sound as though I may be dying with the next cough, and unable to sleep because of the high pitched squealing wheezing sounds I make on the exhale.

Response has been to mainly rest and restore, hoping sleep and time will work its magic. All I know right now is, the last thing I need is to run around getting tests done to find more things going wrong. I don't want to return to a hospital anytime soon, so I refuse to let the doctors back in. I prefer to press on with plans for living and hope for the best.

I suspect this lung purge is a clearing of many things, returning me to the body as it complains that I have ceased caring for it. Like an unloved child, it further breaks down, reminding me to pay more attention, spend more time tuning in and listening to what is truly needed to achieve some new definition of vitality and mobility.

I have arrived, late in life, at the realization that I need people regularly in my life – to confuse and confound me, inform me, trust me, help me, amuse me, encourage me, set me straight, scold me, praise me, see and hear me, and ultimately love me. We all need human interaction to truly thrive, although I worry about people who have expectations of me I will not be able to fulfill, fearing I will ultimately disappoint them.

What keeps me going, other than the amazing help that continues to miraculously appear just in the nick of time, is to fine-tune the apartment. I so love the idea of improving on what you have, to create something new, something lovely, functional and inexpensive. Each choice in renovating has made things easier, as the space arranges itself around upcoming needs and possibilities to facilitate further work. I have been thinking of it as my Pyramid, with all worldly possessions ready for retreat from the world where I can just write. Working title for the ever evolving, expanding, constantly considered book is *An Overly Examined Life*.

November 1
validity/invalidity

A Facebook friend, new to my situation, kindly wrote "At least you are alive". I answered: "Sorry to say there are days when this is not the best news".

After weeks of bronchitis and intestinal upsets, I went cold turkey off the pain meds and am left with my ironic, slightly depressed brain to process yet another season of this demanding journey. Several days of withdrawal, uncontrollable crying and howling, and no sleep, but I did it! Now ten days free and the pain is manageable. I miss the productive, opioid-induced euphoria that enabled me to get so much work done in the apartment these past months since returning home, but am glad to see the back of a myriad of harmful side-affects.

I can't ask much of the foot, as I have done everything the surgeon prescribed and it still doesn't hold me up. Physical therapy is once again suspended in hopes of further healing. My daily reality is of an invalid, requiring great effort just to keep up with simple tasks once performed without thought and taken for granted. Things needing doing that I can't do, accumulate. People are only minimally available. It must be hard for humblingly busy folks to imagine my life. I resist making desperate calls for help, preferring instead to just accept and wait, so grateful for the bounty that has already come my way.

The disappointing medical information has me very shut down and agoraphobic. I have no idea when going out again will feel right. My healing, such as it is, happens inside. When I try to go out, I suffer set-backs. Can you continue to bring the world to me for a while longer, until I begin to get a handle on just what the future holds?

November 16
holidaze

As the holidays come crushing upon us, I am scheduled to see a foot specialist next week and all reports from recent tests point to the need for further surgery. At present I am researching opinions and options and grateful for input from physical therapists, body workers and healers of all kinds as well as my surgeon. I remain hopeful some answers will be found and I may once again walk back into life.

What I need most right now is your company, literally your presence ... for a few hours during the afternoon or early evening ... especially coming up to and during the holidays.

So if you live nearby or are visiting New York, and can see a window when you may be able to travel to Grand Street, please email me your availability so I can begin to rely on a schedule where each day is filled with the grace of human contact.

With enduring love and gratitude for all you continue to do,

November 22
thanks to giving

Of all the people you know, I may have the most to give thanks for this Thanksgiving.

Since my January accident, the outpouring of gifts, donations, visits, necessary tasks accomplished on my behalf and all around generosity of time and spirit has been overwhelming. Because of all of you, I still have hope and believe there may actually be a functional result to all these many months of pain and difficulty. Have A Very Happy Thanksgiving !!!!!!!!!!

December 19
xmas giving

Trying to think what I can give for Christmas and realize I have spent the last 11 months flat on my back watching a lot of movies. So here are some suggestions for in-home entertainment as my gift for this year when I have had to learn how to enjoy incarceration and retreat as a lifestyle. Enjoy !! Merry Christmas To All!

Friday Night Lights – all 5 seasons reveal a long, amazingly well-written video novel. Simply wonderful!

Dean Spanley – My special find of the year with Peter O'Toole, Jeremy Northrup, Bryan Brown and Sam Neill. A gem of a little film with an aging Peter O'Toole as a turn of the century father with a love of dogs. Magical realism ensues.

Brassed Off – British miners play brass band with the amazing character actor Pete Postlethwaite and Ewan McGregor. Brilliant.

Doc Martin – series with Martin Clunes as a Cornish village doctor with some strange personality quirks. Delightfully strange and funny.

Another Year – best offering of all the splendid Mike Leigh films.

Emma – Masterpiece Classic with Romola Garai and Johnny Lee Miller – far better than the one with Gwenyth Paltrow.

The Way We Live Now – historical epic with David Suchet.

Rome – HBO mini-series that rocks!

Joan Rivers: A Piece of Work – Joan as she's never been seen before.

Punching The Clown – off-beat LA film featuring the comic-musical stylings of Henry Phillips, an unusual singer/songwriter.

The Other Guys – Will Ferrell in a surprisingly well done comedy.

Mao's Last Dancer – strong drama of the life of a Communist Chinese ballet dancer who defects to the West.

Easy Virtue – based on a Noel Coward play with Jessica Biel and Colin Firth.

The Moon and the Stars – about Italian film-making as the Fascists take over Rome with Jonathan Pryce and Alfred Molina.

And one of the best films ever made: *The King of Masks* – a Chinese treasure.

68.

2012 - Year Two

January 1
the measure of a year

I haven't written to update you since my Christmas and Thanksgiving offerings, but people are kindly asking how it is going .....

I have been in a holding pattern since before Thanksgiving waiting until Jan 11th to see Dr. Sheskia, a highly regarded foot/ankle surgeon, in hopes there will be some sound medical advice as to further surgeries to resolve the inability of my left ankle to bear weight. I hobble around day to day in what feels like interminable not knowing. Still homebound, pain a constant companion, as I try my best to find silver linings in open spaces. Any future-oriented sense of time closes in.

Many people stepped up, over, and beyond, during the holidays and I had lots of wonderful visitors, plenty of good food and support in all kinds of ways. Thanks for your continued interest in my progress after that ill-fated Jan 5, 2011 encounter with a speeding taxi.

It seems quite impossible it has been nearly a year. What began as an emergency, became an enormous ordeal, developed into the hope all would be made right, has blown up into a gigantic unknown supported by an invalid lifestyle. I try my best to focus on what is possible, but the absurdity of the situation challenges my abilities. I find great comfort in the seemingly endless kindness of friends.

January 5
snow globe

At the year anniversary of my accident, I have found answers to questions I never knew to ask. My life became a snow globe and I, the trapped, inactive figure at the whim of capricious shaking from outside elements.

Wednesday, after months of waiting in ignorance and fear, I see Dr. Sheskia, highly regarded by my emergency attending surgeon Dr. McLaurin and other professionals. I have elicited questions from many of you, so will go in armed with as much information and hope as possible. Whatever I am facing in this second year of infirmity, I trust I can continue to count on your support and assistance. It is the many generous and tolerant people in my life who encourage me to overcome the odds and eventually walk again.

I am spending these last few days slowly getting out the donor confirmations I have been so tardy in completing, and immersed in watching all 6 seasons of "Lost", a program I never saw when it was on. Seems appropriate to be 'lost' in the travails of plane crash survivors battling strange forces on an unknown island.

January 12
hopeful surgeon

Update on Jan 11th appointment:
Dr. Sheskier thinks creatively with a generous and hopeful manner and took a lot of time to go over all my tests. He said the emergency surgeons made a heroic effort to save the ankle, but their attempts had, indeed, failed. Without further surgery I will continue to experience pain and difficulty walking.

I see him again in 2 weeks when he will have considered all possibilities and present me with choices. Further surgery is indicated, but just which procedure would be the best for me is still in question.

So another two weeks of waiting is about all I know. The good news is I liked him, as did Faye and Diann who were with me, so I feel I am in good hands.

Meantime, life continues inactive and shut-in, and I am reliant on those with the time and inclination to keep me going with their spirit and generosity. It's hard to believe I am beginning a second year of recovery from a single instant of impact. Time bends one to its demands.

February 2
spoiler alert

Jan 31st appointment with new surgeon canceled at the last minute. He needs more time to consider if I am a candidate for an ankle replacement. Felt like I had been left at the altar. No clue as to how much longer I will have to wait. "They will call me when they have more information".

So, in frustration, I dive into applying words to this time, this experience, this daily attempt at coping with immobility without the focus of a terminal illness or the hope of a timely surgical intervention. I write to you, my choir of angelic supporters, even as so much bad news and disappointment risks losing your continued interest.

The mind rallies with these two thoughts:

1) To continue altering my thinking in order to absorb and accept new information of increased adversity.
2) The sum of a life is not what you have done, but who you have become while doing what you did.

February 10
quick update

Saw surgeon today.

He is negotiating with a company in California to make me a specially ordered custom artificial joint to surgically implant into my ankle. It may take up to six months for this to come to fruition. Encouraging news as far as commitment and hope, but sobering as to time.

Meantime crawling from moment to moment doing what I can, in the elasticity of time.

February 23
in the extension of time

In this past year I've known people who have lost friends, parents, siblings, pets, suffered critical illnesses, dealt with troubled children and/or troubled marriages, lost jobs, broken down with emotional instability, become overwhelmed with their lives, broken limbs and toes, been in vehicle accidents, had joints replaced, endured major and minor surgeries, lost their home, and experienced every kind of challenge life can serve up.

I know this because many incredible people have found time to share with me facts of their lives. This regular meaningful contact has allowed me to recognize the gift of this time, and understand my experience is only one tone in a symphony of human suffering. No matter what your religion, psychological state or economic status, suffering is real. It takes up time. It cannot be reasoned or denied away. It teaches us about life, it challenges our intelligence, it hones our ability to function and overcome. We are reduced to considering humanity as a shared experience and gratefully become part of the moment to moment flow of time, aware, in its fluidity, it will bring change, no matter that it may feel like it's taking forever.

I don't forget we have shared joyous things as well, laughter and warmth, achievements, the blessed bounty of simply being alive balances out the suffering and allows us to keep on moving on.

March 14
swing low ...

I lost an old friend this week, and realize I will not be able to honor him by gathering with his friends to celebrate his remarkable life. Another close friend is undergoing back surgery and, once again, I am unable to help. Going out for any purpose takes a terrible toll, so I never go anywhere unless it is to a medical appointment.

I founder, entering an increasing void, wearing a frayed mask of coping. Loneliness flashes me the bird of distress.

Pain – sometimes mild, usually furious – turns itself against me and laughs in my face. Daily tasks cause difficulty and frustration.
I have entirely lost any sense of who I was before the accident. Life is requiring quite different things from me and I struggle to comply in time to save some shred of integrity and hope.

What am I, if not a wise eye on a unique journey? The only form left to me is written language. I offer my words, when I am unable to join in the world, with love and thanks for your continued support and wishes for a healing resolution.

March 15
a stumble and a strain

Alert!

I lost my balance and fell on the stairs coming home alone from the doctor yesterday. Managed to catch my weight awkwardly before I went down, badly straining the injured foot.

I have learned from this that I am no longer capable of getting up and down the stairs on my own, so I'm sending this to a few of you who may have flexible schedules and might be called upon to accompany me to medical appointments.

It would mean meeting me at home, taking a car service to and from, and seeing me back up the stairs after. There would always be advanced notice and it doesn't happen often. Mostly it would be in the afternoon on a weekday. Can I put you on a this list?

March 25
dates certain

The first of possibly several further surgeries is scheduled for Thursday, April 12th at Hospital for Joint Diseases 301 E. 17th Street NYC. Although they say this is an out-patient procedure, I have arranged to stay overnight and will 'very carefully' return home on Friday, April 13th. And so, the hopeful fix begins ....

April 8
next phase

Happy Easter, again, unbelievably.

Sixteen months later, as I prepare for surgery this coming Thursday April 12th, I am once again aware of how relying on the medical establishment increases my level of chaos and uncertainty. Their idea of care is not always in sync with my needs. Won't know till the day before, what time I am expected to get to the hospital, but Debra and Diann are covering me. I am expected to return home the next day, Friday the 13th. Dana tells me this is a lucky women's empowerment day. Tracey mentions black cats and ladders.

I will need as much help as I can get over the weekend, as I don't know how much more difficult it will be for me to get around. Not looking forward to increased pain demanding increased medication, but they say this first repair surgery is a matter of six weeks healing. Since I can't put any weight on that foot anyway, things may not be so different.

It is always such a lift to receive visitors who remind me life goes on all around me, although I remain in a holding pattern.

I ask forgiveness for my lack of individual contact. Everything each of you has done on my behalf is etched on my memory with solid strokes.

April 18
to the troops

I have an image of each of us, struggling through our multi-demanding lives, encased in bubble wrap, protection for all that is asked of us day to day, from our families, our work, our challenges, our choices – the things we must do, the things we need to do, the things we do for others, the things that stump us and stop us, the things that propel us onward and reward us.

Each of you have, within your own complicated lives, found time over these post-accident months to keep up with me and many of you have done so much more. I long to send an entry in this, my 'whining path', saying the situation has improved and I am well on the way to walking again. Truth be told, it just ain't so. If you have heard enough and want off this list, please let me know. I don't want my need to record and share the various details and insights of this journey to seem an intrusion. Just reply with "keep me in your address book, but please remove me from the accident update list". I understand.

Sometimes it's too much to remain in close touch with a life so indeterminably in distress and so out of the loop.

Also I may once again be asking for additional help in the form of donations, Fresh Direct gift cards, and the all-important visits. Home from this last surgery, with more to come, I am having a particularly difficult time covering my frustration with a cloak of grace. It just seems more of the same – pain medication making me sick, pain without making me crazy, as I stumble and crawl around my blessed SoHo cave day after day, week after week, month after month, now into the second year of incapacity, writing about it all for whatever it's worth.

On a final unrelated note: Recently realized I watch golf because it is the only sporting event where the commentators actually use the word "delicate".

April 24
the sweetness of love

With a light-hearted spirit, on the subject of recent lessons learned, I must re-address a few things I thought I had long since resolved and absorbed into lifetime practice – for instance the central part sugar plays in our collective sense of well-being.

From the first, Mark and Jim arrived with cookies and chocolate, and the outpouring of yummy symbols of love began. There have been sumptuous birthday cakes, flans, cannolis, every kind of pie and sweet treat imaginable, home baked sweet breads, muffins, seasonal tarts, even ice cream, loads of every kind of cookie and more chocolate in more forms and flavors than I thought possible. Upon coming home, I found it particularly delicious to greet an early visitor with coffee and some treat or other. It was luscious, it was decadent, it was extreme emotional eating, and, although I have thoroughly enjoyed every crumb and sliver, the damage has been done. No matter what the substance, immediate gratification in excess takes a toll and, although I never thought I would understand the heartache of obesity, things have to change.

I had to buy bigger pants. A body that can't actively exercise for month after month becomes a larger version of its true self.

April 28
arresting development

An offering r.e. past and present. Thoughts always surface. I consider them and then move on if there's nothing to act on. The themes are mostly about the meaning of life, how we learn to navigate our individual realities, what it is I can do to improve mine, and how to keep people and supplies coming. I quickly let go of thoughts that prick open the festering boils of anger and fear unless I am faced with medical intervention. Then I unleash the dragons on everyone near, as the only way I can take charge of my extremely vulnerable situation. No more am I the charmer, doing my utmost to be liked by those who bring more pain and restrictions from questionable solutions to my extreme dilemma. I yell when they hurt me, complain when they are vague, dig in when they fail to be forthcoming.

I call this method of navigating the world "negative assertiveness". I learned it first just after my father died suddenly and I had to fly to Denver to take charge when my sister and mother were devastated. On the return flight, I was the one who fell apart and asked the stewardess if I could change seats to sit by a window with the center seat open, so I could collect myself. There were seats free. I wasn't asking the impossible. When they said no, I went to the back of the plane, sat down on the floor and said "I just buried my father, and am not moving until you accommodate me". I was promptly ushered into first class and pampered and fed all the way.

Negative assertiveness has also saved me when, 20 years ago, I was hospitalized for months due to a failed heart valve replacement and then again, for the recent months in rehab after my January 2011 encounter with that speeding taxi. I don't particularly like myself when this aspect is called upon to take charge, but I have learned to trust it, and try not to be too abusive when engaged in it's rare deployment. I even remember to apologize when the crisis passes.

May 16
no mirror here

I am not a mirror, I'm a backboard. I beg you, when you consider me, not to imagine yourself in my situation, but to use my being to bounce against, bringing you somewhere else, somewhere new. I get how difficult it is to witness another person's hardship and inability over a long period of time as fear of associative contagion rises to the surface.

Please just remember I am still reliant on trusted friends. Now that spring has come, perhaps some of you might feel it possible to once again visit? If there's anything I have learned it is we all have demanding, challenging lives, but it is in the sharing of our individual experiences a higher vibration of living is found. I'm a hungry captive ear, still able to offer a unique and clear perspective on how to navigate the inherent difficulties of living it through. If life has you in its grips – visit a shut-in!

I remain on crutches with a couple of rolling stools upon which to move around the apartment. Since the last surgery I have in-home physical therapy twice a week to begin to articulate the toe. Meantime I await news of the custom total ankle replacement the surgeon is hoping for, but clueless as to any time frame. Happily I am largely off pain medication again, and, as long as I put no weight on the left foot, it's not so bad.

> sometimes I drop into despair
> and measure with what isn't there
> a long dream sleep can peel my eyes
> to see what time has realized
> we rest upon a pile of gifts
> contemplating thoughts that lift
> people come and go and stray
> what they bring remains in play.

June 8
a year later

Stephanie recently observed I have completely re-created my life. I agree, but a re-creation centered on disability is not the way I might prefer to evolve.

It's one year since I returned home with the hope I would begin walking again. As you know, this hope, so celebrated at the lovely City Winery Benefit, was not to be. I saw the surgeon last week and the latest report is they are moving on getting the customized hardware to facilitate the total ankle replacement after six months of waiting. This means the surgical 'fix' may happen before the end of the summer if all goes well. Not sure if many of you realize that since November the condition of the ankle has been deteriorating. What I was able to do last June is now quite impossible. I can't even go up or down the stairs by myself, hence the greater need for folks to accompany me to urgent medical appointments. There will be more of those in the coming weeks, I'm afraid, as the work-ups necessary for a final surgical solution begin to grow.

On a directly hopeful note, Carmen deLavellade has referred me to the Actor's Fund and they are considering my case as one eligible for their help. Not sure what this means, but all forms of support are a blessing.

Many reliable, available friends are going out of town this summer leaving me a bit more in need of on-site help. Please check your schedule and try to offer me an afternoon or evening when you might stop by and bring the world in to my functional SoHo survival cave. Your stories of interaction with the outside world inspire me and keep me hopeful for a day I may once again re-create my life centered on increased ability and creative strength.

July 9
fresh direct appeal

Email updates have become increasingly difficult to draft. This is because I have no news. I am into the 7th month of waiting for an ankle replacement, hostage to a surgeon's promises, still home-bound. My sense of time and reality is deeply compromised, as I must constantly create ways to survive and cope with disability and pain, not knowing when or what or how the future will present change. Some days It feels as though I'm losing the battle.

Yours in the spirit of anything is possible ...

July 16
glimpses of clarity

Some days I awake with clarity. It's as though a veil has lifted and I can see what it is I am to do, having shed the heavy mantel of post-accident recovery. All thoughts of what I've endured and will still, have skittered to the corners, out of sight. I arise and begin the tasks of daily renewal. Water is filtered and poured into the kettle to heat for coffee, dishes are washed or sorted, online the email is checked for immediate response need and weather is checked so I know how to monitor the interior climate control. I think about what I will need to ask someone to do for me this upcoming week, and carefully tend the small embers of what may be possible. I do not cling to thoughts, but allow them to float to the surface and act upon them if I can.

Then I think about the people I am blessed to have in my life and how and when to contact them via phone or email. These past six months of near stasis in my healing process have taken a toll, since I have no news of a positive nature to share. I think about the differing lives my friends each lead and the challenges and difficulties they continue to face. I mourn my own losses, wonder if I will ever re-occupy my body with a sense of vitality and purpose, sometimes cry as someone tells me of their physical regimen demonstrating a great facility for living.

Piles of 'considerations' surround me. Snail correspondence from a lifetime, career archives that continue to accumulate with little focus or forward intention for sharing, so many clothes & shoes (many of which I will probably never wear again, but don't want to cut until I have a sense of what kind of life I'm heading towards), a kitchen of supplies collected over a lifetime, too many books, and an excess of papers to sort and cut and eliminate. Just running technology's obstacle course of changing format year in and year out over a 34 year career is a frustrating challenge.

These are the times this writing voice insists itself, so I sit and attempt to capture my experience in language to convey some sort of useful meaning to others.

I do what I can – and then retreat into my ongoing marathon of watching movies and videos, where past performances live through time.

September 29
endless fail

I have just re-read my missives to you (averaging 3 a month) since "not yet walkin" March 22, 2011 – 2 months after being hit by that cab on January 5, 2011. In addition to keeping you informed about how I was coping with a jagged twist of fate, these regular emails have given me a voice, a way of being present in your lives when circumstances prevented my being physically in the world. I haven't written since "glimpses of clarity" July 16, 2012.

You may have hoped my silence indicated a change in my situation, perhaps for the better, however I am sad to report no real change is possible until I undergo a promised ankle replacement. My surgeon now says it may be January before surgery can be scheduled. No other reason is forthcoming beyond "it takes as long as it takes". If recent timeline is to be believed, I will have turned 70 by the time they finally come up with a viable solution – two years after the initial accident. I deteriorate daily, still unable to walk, doing the best I can to live as a shut-in and maintain essential upkeep. I have chosen a path of non-struggle, less pain medication, rather than forcing efforts to be further in the world.

A few stalwart angels check in on me regularly. Paid angels work weekly to cover house-keeping and laundry. Basic needs are miraculously being met, but my strength to keep it all coming has changed. I have tapped my reserves, over-extended my abilities. Beyond daily tasks of food and upkeep I have little idea who I am or what it is I am to do. The past has been erased and the future exists as a multiple choice test of fearful unknowns. I remain in a sort of time stasis, where nothing seems to make a difference by offering the hope of further healing. Even so, when I look at the big picture, aware of what everyone must deal with in our complex lives, there is much to be grateful for.

Some days I don't know how I can continue, and then Suellen comes with seared tuna for Sunday dinner or Diann brings turkey and funny stories of how it is to be part of the world. David and Jean send Yana (a Russian physical therapist who treats Cindy Sherman) to help me reclaim the use of my right arm due to shoulder problems. Calls come from Jake and Tim, Carmen and Valda, emails from out of town – Debra and Katherine and Sue and Cheryl and Traer. Joshua and Diane take time to punch up my computer. Pat turns up after a year of changing her life completely. Marie brings baklava and lovely photos of India. Old friends include me in rare New York City visits. Stephanie still comes once a week without fail for an after work Happy Hour. Every so often I have a marathon 'consult' with JoAnn, one of my closest friends. I rely on massage therapy with Michele, and Diann's Alexander expertise to help me make feeble attempts at reclaiming my ruined body. Written notes of cheer and donations still arrive, as well as the all-important gift certificates to Fresh Direct.

I am looking at another holiday season homebound. How strange it is to have not left my apartment, except for doctor's appointments, in all these months. I wish I could tell you I have become so enlightened over this long ordeal, I am detached from the pain and frustration. Dream on!

As I perceive what is happening in the human carnival around me, I key onto loss and disappointment, trust and validation, truth and cover-up. How much we want others to perceive us as different than we perceive ourselves to be. How our desire for power over our own lives drives us to dress ourselves up in some way our intellect deems acceptable to those we seek to impress. How each of us is deeply touched by an often overwhelming sense of loss. How difficult it is to bear repeated disappointments as we make efforts to navigate through. How challenging is the need to share real circumstances that are uniquely awful. How elusive is the truth of our own existence and the acceptance of what can validate us enough to attempt the struggle to go on. How futile our puny efforts too often seem.

I keep going through thoughts of the myriad individual kindnesses and vast generosity each of you have offered over this long time of trial. Please make some time to visit now that we are into fall and the weather has improved. Regular human contact makes all the difference.

October 11
mewling puddle

I encourage your visits. Though still homebound, I remain lucid and a listening ear, hungry for the blessing of human contact. Moving into nearly two years of incapacity, visitors often ask me "How is it you are not a mewling puddle on the floor, curled up in the fetal position at this point?"

It is a matter of quieting down the areas of my mind that vibrate with nervousness, often about nothing known.

I get through by:

- accepting the truth of my experience.
- bringing my mind to the moments, paying attention to each detail of perception as it presents itself.
- setting aside some of what is known, in favor of what one can possibly do something about, now.
- letting go of whatever ultimately can't be helped.
- addressing physical pain with movement.
- remembering the generosity and kindness of people.
- laughing at the ironies and tragedies in our lives.
- an ultimate belief in the strength to endure, for whatever is next in store for us.

Of course every so often the pain drives me to cry and scream like a torture victim just to purge the system. I think that helps, too.

October 25
facts in time

My surgeon, Dr. Steven Sheskier, has at last called with the following information.

He just signed off on the final design for a new Total Ankle Replacement after detailed consultation with a team of surgeons who have been considering my case all these months. It is a special custom implant which has not been formerly available, hence the long delay.

Now begins another long process involving the actual manufacture of the new TAR, final ok by the surgical board of the Hospital for Joint Diseases, and approval by Medicare. At this stage they do not foresee any major impediments.

However, we are now looking at another six months at least for all this to come to pass.

So once again I must rely on your continuing support. Managing a life on remote control has been a considerable challenge. I hope your help with this daunting task will be there to get me through yet another holiday season, my 70th birthday in January, and the deepening promise of another major surgery sometime in the spring accompanied by resultant months of rehab and recovery in a sort of deja vu of post-traumatic stress.

I remain overwhelmed by your contributions, anonymous and otherwise. The plethora of kind gestures and investments in my life have enabled me to keep facing this endurance test.

November 3
let there be

Post-Sandy, I have moved from desperate, back down to needy as the power came on at 5 o'clock this morning after going out completely all at once around 8:30 Monday evening; five days of the darkest dark I can remember.

I had no access to email or cell phone, but somehow was able to access an old land-based phone line with no electric components, so could be in contact with a few of you. Stephanie once again bailed me out with a heroic dash into NY from Brooklyn with ice and a cooler, candles, an extra flashlight and matches. Debra and Suellen, also in the dark, but mobile, took care of increasing needs as the days went on. Jean found me the first day, but then was able to get out of town and spend the post hurricane insanity upstate with David.

I was one of the lucky ones, since I had cold water, the gas heater and stove. I also had essential food, left the refrigerator and freezer closed, but lost all the carefully collected frozen things, so will need to restock. Local stores and restaurants were in the same boat, so it will be a few days before I can access deliveries.

Thank God for WNYC, our local radio station who ran 24/7 on FM on a generator in spite of also being in the blackout area. I had a battery operated portable radio to keep me company the whole time, so was able to listen to the moving stories of so many who lost lives and homes. Now the affected neighborhoods are digging out from a terrible toll. Our deepest humanity is revealed at times like this as people are banding together and helping those in need.

December 17
cry for help

I think about sending a Xmas upbeat list of my picks for movies, like last year, but seem to have lost some of my strength of spirit.

Truth is, my inner lights never came back on after Sandy. It was sort of the last straw. Oh, I am still here, coping with a situation where I experience no improvement or healing, only painful physical deterioration and an increasing inability to move, waiting for an alleged ankle replacement (which is beginning to sound delusional), looking at my 70th birthday on January 15th.

I have, with a lot of angelic help for nearly two years, managed to find ways to survive and remain hopeful but, after so many have done so much to keep me going in all sorts of ways, I'm sorry to report I am losing this waiting game – running out of available friends, projected funds, creative functioning ideas.

The only new truth that glimmers through is – without the ability to experience change, endurance seems futile.

Please reach me, in whatever way you can. As strong as my mind has remained through this, I have reached a pass where I frankly don't know what to do with this growing belief I will never reclaim an active productive life.

I am no less reminded of the myriad acts of generosity and kindness that have come my way over this long, long time.

December 31
bye bye 2012

In bidding farewell to a year that offered me a rare opportunity to evolve through adversity, mostly I have all of you to thank for getting me through.

Formal thankyous for some specific gifts ....
- Donations to my non-profit The Corporeal Studio Ltd. and gift certificates to Fresh Direct.
- Some of you have actually sent cash through the mail and cash is the easiest for me to put to use, so massive thanks to those who have risked the pitfalls of the post office.

- Each and every phone call, message, letter, card and email letting me know you thought of me.
- So many surprise packages from smoked salmon and a subscription to the New Yorker to lavender oil, a harmonica, Burt's Bees lip gloss, books, DVD's and a myriad of edible goodies.
- I'll never forget the flowers you sent and brought. I am careful to dry as many as possible and so always have dried arrangements if not always fresh flowers to cheer my survival cave.
- Every visit has been the boost I've needed to carry on. I am beyond grateful to those of you who took time in your busy lives for a periodic stop-over to my little Grand Street apartment.
- To those who arrived at Grand Street with shopping and supplies, food and meals, candles and batteries during the black out, taking on tasks of trash out, mail in and out, your combined efforts have enabled me to keep up with keeping going.

I have learned about endurance, acceptance, shifting focus onto what is possible instead of focusing on what has been lost, and the inherently deep value of friendship. I remain hopeful that Dr. Sheskier will, sometime in 2013, find a solution to my devastated ankle and offer me another chance to suffer surgery, recovery and ultimate healing, enabling mobility once again.

The folks on this list have made all the difference. There are not thankyous enough for your generosity, sensitivity, compassion and trust. Best to all in 2013 !!!

PART III – LESSONS LEARNED
A KIND OF HEALING

69.

2013 – Year Three

January 18
regarding birthdays

As some of you know, I turned 70 January 15th. I wish I could have hired a hall and thrown a big bash, but my homebound condition allowed just a small gathering with wine and cake. Circumstances these past two years have made me largely absent from the world outside Grand Street and from the lives of many people I value

Life As We Know It At 70

Sometimes sleeping, usually not
distractive actions at the ready
rising to a coffee pot
and something sweet to keep me steady

neti, pedi, stretch and scream
pot the plant, plot the mind
analyze a frequent dream
minimize what turns me blind

maximize the exercise
hobble, stumble, lurch and drop
kill the doubt, open eyes
avoid a constant thought to stop

people come and people go
bringing blessed human kind
other is often all I know
as days begin, proceed, unwind

computerize online to shop
folks deal with mail, dump my trash
food arrives before I flop
saving me from a total crash

don't forget to supplement
the non-prescription way to heal
dozens of doses of pills are sent
to strengthen and add to the daily meal

I've redefined my sense of time
nothing happens when I want
accepting this extended crime
is cruel and hard and tough and blunt

I haven't dealt with what is lost
too much, too deep, too sad, too scary
mundanity defines my days
and wary friends both dare and spare me

so many people seem to care
I write to you, through dark and cold
from my cave, my womb-like lair
in spite of all ... I don't feel old.

February 4
expanding contact

If you are receiving this, you are on my 'accident update' list. It was begun after I was hit by a cab in January of 2011 – a series of factual and expansive writings about this journey of two years trying to walk again. I send about 1-3 each month. This month I have added folks who have recently contacted me via Facebook or who mean a lot to me and may not know about my situation.

As of now, I am still homebound awaiting a promised ankle replacement with date uncertain. Please reply to this email with 'remove' in the subject line if you wish to be removed from the list. I do understand. All of our lives are deeply challenging, complicated and often overwhelming.

But it is the kind folks on this list who have been my life-line to the world. Someone here saves me every day as I am unable to show up for outside events, meetings and a social life.

April 22
disparate spring thoughts

Haven't written in a while. Please set this aside for when you have the time. It's just a couple of snaps on my current mind-set

The Balance Factor
Overall balance is so hard to find. If it isn't one thing, it's another. I may awake clear-headed, but then engage in the simplest of upright tasks only to find I am huffing and puffing for air and quite exhausted. Or a runny nose presumably from allergies becomes a full blown nose bleed requiring half an hour of pressure and ice to finally stop. I begin to doubt I will ever emerge from this cave of inactivity. How close are the connections of body/mind/spirit? We must work on all of them in order to find balance.

The Pain Factor
Pain often comes upon us in mysterious ways, an attack of burning or stabbing or aching that seems to come from no known cause. We throw everything at it – and when nothing works we then try leaving it alone. More often than not, sleep grants ease. Sometimes it takes days of endurance. Then we wake one day and it has passed. A good

215

day becomes a day without pain. Activities are chosen by their ability to either take our mind off the pain or to actually address it with drugs or applications. We try this and that, paying attention to what seems to help. With cause and effect in mind, we curtail choices that seem to instigate it and keep trying to choose towards lessening.

The doctors would treat it with drugs, the enlightened with meditation, the physical therapists with exercise, the psychotherapists with a reconsideration of our emotional archaeology. Can it be treated with acceptance and escape?

The Emotion Factor
Some kind of unknowable awareness rules the emotional life. It takes over when the logic of 'normal' requires us to behave in certain socially acceptable ways. We resist. A necessary distance emerges. We trust more in our own sensibilities than in what may be expected of us. We will not doubt our inner self. We can't, even to save our lives, because, in the end, it is really all we have.

The Friend Factor
It's gone way past not getting my needs met – it's as though I no longer know what my needs are. Human relationships are a constant challenge and fascination. Having friends in our lives depends on remembering the power of thought, and the limits of action. Connections can lift us up or bring us down – it's our choice which can happen.

April 28
rare and gifted journeys

Spring brings a peeling off. Layers of doubt and fear seem to fade into haze as I gingerly crawl back into my body. Still no ankle fix. I have been waiting so long, focused on the promise of a viable joint upon which to rebuild. But there is a limit to placing one's trust in an unknown future resolve. Instead, I must accept this extended delay and try to improve existence within.

Most important is to renew my conversation with my body. It has become so foreign to me, so lost. I have been ignoring all but its most pressing needs for nourishment and basic exercise. I think of all the victims of the Boston bomb and the soldiers coming home from wasted wars without limbs. We must open our sense of self to give greater value to the parts we can't see – the spirit, the soul, the willpower and resolve that can come by embracing and integrating life forces swirling beneath our emotional and mental fragility.

Those who have been dancers recognize, as we grow older, there is a greater calling our deep physical understanding can employ to carry us to the next place on this rare and gifted journey.

May 28
portrait of waiting

Time is a healing balm, requiring patience to apply.

Suffering appears and disappears at regular intervals. Perhaps it is always here and what wavers is the choice to make it visible and felt.

This body has been so altered, so compromised, so crushed. I don't recognize what was once my primary conduit to reality. I haul it around as best I can. If I exert a bit too much effort in the rehabilitation process, I pay for it with increased pain, so I do as little as possible to keep going. I'm still stuck in a gap of limited progress prior to additional surgery.

Sometimes I can address the environment and make changes adding some grace and ease to the days, but only with help from others. When someone comes to visit, they help me accomplish what would be impossible on my own. My days are scheduled around these blessed visits as I try to be present when someone is here, attempt to offer what I am able, and appreciate a precious life force freely given.

There are acts I think to do, but ideas deflate in the face of current reality. Unknowns have infested my brain and knocked out motivation. I seem to have lost all threads to work. Still, I process, though it rarely leads to creation.

I would love to have deep conversations with certain individuals, but may never get the chance. I mourn those who couldn't take in all I must demand of them and so have disappeared, leaving a strong awareness of loss in their wake.

Larger subjects such as giving and receiving love seem to have been tabled indefinitely beyond the affection of friendship.

I rarely descend into despair, but the face of my suffering leers at me with disdain and challenge. Instead of licking that face, I usually turn away towards acceptance and distraction. But to hold up a mirror to despair and share the ugly image from time to time seems to help. Forgive me.

July 8
thanks and news

Good news! I received an extensive call from my surgeon Dr. Steven Sheskier responding to my growing concerns. He seems to believe a satisfactory solution will be realized and assures me the delay has been because of the uniqueness of my case and the creative impetus to invent a new kind of ankle implant. He leads me to believe this choice will ultimately be the right one and another long period of healing may result in full mobility. I continue to wait for this surgery to be scheduled, remaining deeply grateful for those of you who have expressed concern with my well-being.

In the meantime, watching loads of movies supplies me with the occasional choice quote to share:

from *Cloud Atlas*:

"Our lives are not our own,
from womb to tomb we are bound to others, past and present,
and by each crime and every kindness we give birth to our future".

September 2
labored exercise

Here it is Labor Day and I'm still laid up with no info about the elusive ankle replacement. I have adapted to a strange life, involving way too much thinking and not nearly enough doing.

I occasionally find myself in a bit of a chuckle about just how I manage to get around this apartment with a missing ankle bone on the left side and an arthritic hip on the right. Mainly slow and steady as she goes and constantly bringing my awareness to the moment, avoiding a trip or a slip or a fall that might create more loss. Much sitting, teetering, lounging and scooting.

I have been blessed with a few amazingly generous and loyal friends who keep me company, bring me supplies, help with what I cannot do, and, most of all, bring love – their love of life, family, work and struggle. Although I am lax in not contacting each of you individually, I remain open to visitors whenever your busy lives may bring you to SoHo. I try to respond to all emails, and, with a day's notice, can be available most anytime, any day.

I count myself lucky to have your support and the glimmer of hope that one day I will find medical answers to this nearly three years of incapacity.

October 5
into another fall?

Here it is October 2013 and I still occupy my 'fortress of solitude.' (Grabbed from the original Christopher Reeve Superman. "He walked into the Fortress of Solitude and, after a few years, learned what he needed to know in order to fly out").

News from my surgeon is "We hope to get this done before the end of the year". Denia, his practice manager, tells me in 16 years of working with Dr. Sheskier she has never actually seen medical history being made – from the imagination of a brilliant surgeon's desire to specifically address my unique injury, through the entire process of obstacles getting FDA approval to the actual design process, manufacture process and all the other necessary 'oks', this is going to be a definite first. Will it have been worth waiting years for? We shall see.

Meantime I have lost my functional edge of growing old with grace, and play hurry up, catch up with all the other systems keeping me going – heart, lungs, digestion – none of them thriving on serious long-term immobility. The only system to remain somewhat reliable is my mind, thanks to the contact and support from all of you. You keep me a little bit saner, a lot more comfortable, increasingly humble and determined to made this thing work so I can return to a life where I can actually 'show up' from time to time. Fingers crossed for a fortunate outcome.

October 31
halloween again already …

Just when I feel my mind's rabid hound nipping at my heels with "how have you allowed your life to come to this pass?" I confront the dogs of self-war with "you are not real – judging me is just another dodge!"

Managing to very carefully, with extreme effort, get down on the floor and do a little yoga. I have kept up certain restorative poses I can do on the bed, but word is the floor will offer more resistance and ultimately prove more beneficial. Slow going, but still haven't returned to pain meds. Challenges abound. As expected, no word from surgeon's office after hopeful last report.

Loss of cultural heroes like Lou Reed (just a year older than me) widen the void. However, like the Dude, I continue to 'abide' as the weather grows cold once again.

Think of me as the Holidays approach with their usual emotional sledge hammer, and blessings on you and yours.

December 5
thanksgiving pulse

As the 2013 Holidays commence, ribbons of thought, one after another, unfurl to consciousness.

As much as I would like to achieve an overall peace of extreme enlightenment, feeling OK moment to moment seems to be the highest ideal to which I can aspire. All other desires eventually find ragged fulfillment in an internet shopping capability and the hands-on efforts of a few good friends.

Momentary lifts come in the form of lovely food, flowers and way too many sweets. I monitor my chemical balance by staying off pain medication and take a slew of supplements daily. Each time I stand, it is a challenge to see how I might be able to make it from one room to the other with the least amount of discomfort. I have rolling stools and chairs for times when my legs simply fail to hold me up.

Mostly I think about how I could be doing better. The human drive to improve oneself, to make evolving moments grow stronger as they disappear one into the next, never goes away. I berate an inability to access disciplines, overcome infirmity, make truer, more ircumspect choices. The duo of pain and time play a symphony of thinking. I claim small joys: visits from the few folks who still check in on me and help from time to time; a movie or tv show to make me laugh or satisfy a deep craving for drama, for differing points of view, for creative crafting of words and images capable of challenging my mind and urging it to press on.

And I think about all of you and how your multiple acts of kindness and generosity have eased my way. Seasonal thanks for your ongoing heroic attempts to help keep me on the planet,

December 24
video picks from 2013

Whether it's Merry Christmas or some other celebratory greeting, I wish you ease and relief and comfort for this winter season of holidaze. Here is a list of some favorite offerings I found on video in 2013. Enjoy!

Defiance – WWII Bella Russe with Liev Shreiber and Daniel Craig as brothers who save over a thousand Jews from the Nazis by living in the woods.

The Sapphires – 1960's Aboriginal Australian girl singing group travels to Viet Nam to entertain the troops.

The English Teacher – Julianne Moore, a high school teacher whose former student returns having written a play, and wants their high school to produce it. With Nathan Lane and Greg Kinnear.

Frances Ha – off-beat black and white film about a young girl struggling to make it in New York as a modern dancer.

Stories We Tell – Sarah Polley's brilliant offering and totally original style of dramatized documentary.

Not Fade Away – Teen rock group grows up. With James Gandolfini as the father – a nostalgic study of the 60's.

Gideon's Daughter – with Bill Nighy, Miranda Richardson and Emily Blunt, the first and best of Director Steven Poliakoff's Trilogy of a crumbling capitalistic culture. Others are *Almost Strangers* and *Friends and Crocodiles.*

The World's End – Simon Pegg in a mid-life-crisis pub crawl that goes horribly wrong.

The Man Who Sued God – Judy Davis and Billy Connelly – high comedy with a twist.

Songs from the Second Floor – strange surreal film unlike any other.

Lilies – 3 part Irish series of 3 sisters finding how to thrive after WWII in Dublin with a widowed father and the returning soldiers reclaiming their jobs.

Super 8 – JJ Abrams writes and directs this nod to producer Steven Spielberg of a group of teenagers shooting their own movie only to discover something exceedingly strange.

The Cabin in the Woods – all-time favorite writer/director Joss Whedon's take on horror.

Centurion – 2nd Century Britain and Roman soldier Michael Fassbender combine to make this a memorable offering by director Neil Marshall.

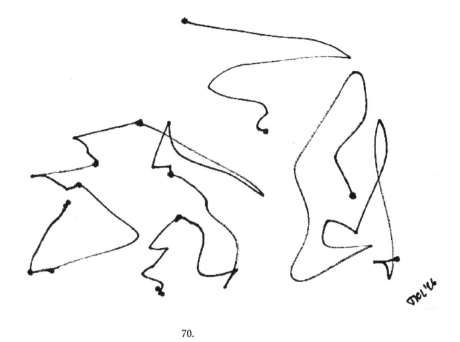

70.

2014 - Year Four

February 7
jade rabbit

All celebratory excuses have passed with the Seattle Super Bowl a distant memory of yesterday's news. Like the Chinese Jade Rabbit on the moon, disfunction compels me to communicate my predicament.

When faced with 'what to do next' I ruminate on aspects of living like 'choice' and 'time' and 'love' and wax philosophical.

Aspiration and motivation have been erased with the wet rag of incapacity. As I manage life in remote control, I can only hope sometime in the months to come, I will begin another phase of this journey and have some much needed good news to share.

I count blessings along the way such as having access to good food, control of my own heat, the computer and online shopping, a constant supply of interesting videos, the ongoing tasks of organizing paper work and putting written affairs in order. Visits always get top priority. If someone has scheduled to come, I make the brave effort to be available and relatively cleaned up. But often I am afraid of the road I am on. All I can see is more pain and hospitalization and long months of rehab, even if the work can be scheduled. Other than that, I pour myself into writing it all down, attempting to bring into focus some organizing principle through which to process all the words I have generated as a portrait of this pass in my lifetime. Without the obsession to write my story and pass on a glimmer of appreciation to those who care, I would have been lost entirely.

I fear my plight has become a burden to some of you and am sorry for that. Going through all the wonderful cards and letters you have showered upon me during these now 3 years of an upended apple cart reminds me many of you are thinking of me still. Visits always appreciated.

Yours in the spirit of gratitude and determination,

April 2
cultivating change

Thanks to all for the spring Fresh Direct donations. Much appreciated.

As I continue this waiting game, time passing offers very small, infrequent changes. When I detect a change for better or worse, I consider how and what and where it may have sprung from. I cultivate change like caring for a tenuous fire of small embers in an attempt to keep something going. This remains my central job – adopting a demeanor of mindful consideration in the moments of each day as I taste whatever life I can find. How it continues to feel and the way everything has been altered by this experience, is thrown into process. Once I find a realization of cause/effect, challenge/resolve, I usually feel quite full of hope. It lasts until the next bout of pain attacks and I am once again fighting bitter symptoms. I gave up on pain medications months ago. The mask was not worth the side-effects.

When moving my body, I proceed with extreme caution. Any off-sided or stressful move will bring pain or even further injury. I walk a tightrope of careful unsteady stepping from point to point. Slow moves become an analysis of alignment with pain as the guide. More than three years of this has taken a toll. I no longer recognize my own body. If I do too much, pain ensues. If I do too little, pain ensues. Vibrating at this low level, at this slow speed, often feels quite impossible.

I am constantly aware so many of you have your own challenges and the cumulative stress can be daunting. As to these words I am sharing with you, I seek to sculpt language that may reveal a deeply embedded and tested process for surviving a continuing challenge. May we all endure our difficulties with grace and gratitude.

From the mundane to the ridiculous – through to the sublime.

April 24
spring bounty

Many of you have expressed concern for my quality of life, being largely homebound the past 3 1/2 years. Fortunately my mind has remained sound enough to focus on what is possible and not dwell on what has been lost. The biggest challenge was learning how to manage life while never going out – getting food and supplies delivered, arranging apartment upkeep and laundry, paying bills, preparing meals – all with the help of kind, generous, hard-working folks. My usual solitary functioning has of necessity become reliant on others. Visits are the highlights of my days.

I've discovered patience, acceptance, appreciation for small things and have let go of any need to succeed or compete. Until I regain mobility I am in retreat and, surprisingly, find there a state of grace. I've discovered one can tap into a moment to moment kind of life force, even though I miss showing up and witnessing the changing of the seasons.

In this apartment (where I have lived since 1978) everywhere you look, from any angle, there are interesting shapes and colors and evidence of a vital and intelligent life, a living installation, a perfect construction of function and meaning. I remain perpetually aware of work to be done and balance to be reached for, but my time is my own and I have been blessedly relieved of the additional stress of outside deadlines and responsibilities.

Pain, however, seems to be the elephant in the room. It is the body's most intimate language, understood only by the person in pain. Heard a victim of the Boston Marathon bombing say living with constant pain is an unimaginable stressor and amputation of an injured limb may perhaps be a better solution than saving it at all costs. Sanity is the awareness there are always options.

June 3
hip first

I finally saw the ankle surgeon who brought in his hip guy. Decision has been made to replace the right hip before replacing the left ankle.

So I am now gearing up for hip replacement surgery.

June 17
volunteers needed

My old friend Pat Graf recently emailed me: "I was intrigued to think those of us on your mailing list belong to an exclusive club of sorts; we are united in a community ... and the link we all have in common is you. All of us are now less alone".

Thanks Pat, for the lovely thought.

As to the developing details of upcoming hip replacement surgery, the operation is scheduled for July 8th with Dr. Edward Adler and will be performed at The Hospital for Joint Diseases on 2nd Ave at 17th St. My ankle surgeon believes I can rehabilitate the right hip without the use of the left ankle, however I won't know if I qualify for in-patient physical therapy until after the surgery. The next 3 weeks I may have to get out to appointments with various doctors, as yet unscheduled.

Several of my most reliable help will be out of town much of the rest of June and after surgery in July. If you might be available to accompany me to necessary Dr. appts. in preparation for surgery, or to help either at the hospital or at home after, please let me know. I do not yet have specific dates, but hope to compile a list of those who might be in town and free, with the hope a few will be able to spend time with me.

July 7
new chapter

Hip replacement taking place on schedule Tuesday morning, July 8th at 10am at Hospital for Joint Diseases 17th St and 2nd Ave NYC.

Will not be in further contact with everyone until I know where I will be after 3-4 days there. Assuming all goes well, I hope to be admitted to a sub-acute rehab facility for as long as it takes for the hip to once again hold me up. After being confined to this apartment for 3½ years, leaving it for an indeterminate amount of time is challenging.

Thanks for keeping me going. One of you saves me in some way every day, week, month, year of this long ordeal.

May love and grace surround you until we are once again in contact.

July 15
landed

Thanks for all the well wishes before and during new surgery. So far, so good.

I am currently at Village Care sub-acute rehab facility at 214 West Houston Street, New York, NY 10014 for a minimum of twenty days with option to extend if necessary.

You can phone 646-380-7047 to reach me directly, but I won't be making calls out. I only have a simple pay-as-you-go cell phone for emergencies.

"A tiny image of my body floats into and out of the heart with each breath, and I imagine deep healing." (Thanks to Carol Mann for the meditation imagery)

August 2
coping at home with a new hip

Except for the small group of 30 who were included in this last hospitalization period, you haven't heard from me. I discovered, once in rehab, I couldn't send group emails from the iPad, so the one you got with my location and contact info was sent by inputting each of 300 names individually! It was truly a labor of love ...

227

Came home Fri, Aug 1st and found apartment in great shape. Was so glad to sleep in my own bed again. Life pretty much as it was except the hip pain is from surgery and rehab instead of the unpredictable and awful arthritis. This is truly an amazing thing they can do – to take away all those years of arthritis pain and give us new hips.

So once again the future lies in the hands of the ankle surgeon, Dr. Steven Sheskier, whenever the hip is healed and I am ready for the much anticipated ankle implant. May the powers that be, finally overcome the delays and grant us a short next period of waiting for the last and final surgery to put me back on my legs.

Once again many thanks for all gifts, cards and calls, and for your continued interest and concern. I am truly blessed to know each and every one of you and to have been relying on your kindness and generosity these many years since my unfortunate run-in with that cab.

August 28
hip hip hooray

Saw the hip surgeon yesterday and everything is healing on schedule. Getting stronger on that leg every day. A great relief to be free of arthritic pain. Ankle, of course, remains non-viable, so homebound status ongoing.

Can't believe it is nearly Labor Day leading to my fourth fall season of injury/repair lifestyle.

Thanks for everything you have done and continue to do to help me make sense of it all.

September 14
autumnal prep

September is often lost in resolving the summer and preparing for fall. Then October hits us as the beginning of the dreaded "Holidaze" – nearly 4 months of emotionally draining events featuring unsatisfied long-yearned-for needs and crippling regrets, coupled with an uptake in socialization and a deep need for loving friends.

Reaching out has grown harder and harder. I have efficiently figured out how to take care of material maintenance, but the intellectual and emotional needs are hungry. I am loathe to appeal to people, knowing how complicated everybody's lives seem, unless it is an emergency. There have been enough of those and many stepped up. But most folks barely have time for the principle people in their lives – namely their families. There is a tribal core that protects and supports those closest to us. When so few are close and those few rarely available, it is a problem. People drift away, forget, give up on the long endurance runs that overtake some of us.

I am still eternally grateful for all the kindnesses and contact, but am deeply lonely. I can't seem to turn this into blessed solitude anymore. I am surprised at how much I now need people – not for what they can do for me, but for their being, their otherness, their own soul's journey shared. Looking at four years of being whisked away from autonomy in the world, to a certain level of autonomy out of the world and I find myself bereft. Loss has become a way of life leading nowhere.

When weighing the advantages and disadvantages of our humanity, I realize person to person communication is pretty much the crux of it.

I write my mind – and, as I read what I write, see how troubled I have become. These ruminations are a dangerous mobius strip that seem perpetual – like the Cosmic War we have been pulled into. It will not end until something is eliminated and there's no way of knowing what that may be.

October 6
actionable intelligence

Recent response to my 'cry for help' confirms that asking for what we need works. After several long phone conversations, a few timely visits, a slew of email correspondence, I once again feel as though I can do this.

Hip continues to hold me up with little pain. As to the question everyone asks "any news on the ankle replacement?" My surgeon is ready to schedule the surgery for February. Yay! But it's a little like booking the wedding after a long, difficult engagement – an act not free from trepidation!

Meantime there are the dratted holidays to limp through. I'm still in this fight for full mobility and, with your continuing help, hope to find the strength.

November 20
another needy thanksgiving

Strange how a memory of what cold feels like isn't retained. We are always taken a bit by surprise when it hits again.

You have not heard from me for a while. In my case, no news is exactly that – no news. Back to waiting with nothing definite as to final surgery.

But this is the season of giving thanks and I will never be able to adequately express the deep gratitude I feel for how much has come my way in these past years of difficulty.I do wish the need were less, but it seems to grow rather than diminish. Sadly I have lost contact with many of you. I understand this is part of a long evolution of change, but I miss those with whom I had been close. Regardless of distance, I continue to hold each of you in my heart and am in awe of those who regularly show up.

The good news is I'm mostly ambulatory much of the time, and manage to get myself from room to room with some ease and little pain. Tackling the stairs is still too much, but I get on the upright bike for 20 minutes a day most days now, and dutifully keep up with the exercise program created after the July hip replacement. I have stopped consuming sugar except honey, maple syrup and fruit, and am eating a variety of good food easily prepared in small portions. I can now stand well enough to make a meal each evening and am finding that improving one's taste is the best way to diet.

It is some sort of miracle to have emerged from violent trauma mentally able to put a few thoughts together. However, my dogged attempt to reawaken the body after all this down time, is a big climb. The course is clear, but the mind not lways. Sometimes I lose the will to carry on, but then some blessed act of kindness comes my way and the energy shifts.

December 19
holiday watcher's list

In the Spirit of the Season, here is my yearly video watcher's suggestion list. Enjoy!

(Series with 2021 update)

Longmire – Netflix streaming – 6 Seasons complete – 2012-2017
Modern western based on novels by Craig Johnson – Native American theme.

Peaky Blinders – Netflix streaming – 7 seasons complete– 2013-2022
Powerful Irish gang in London turn of the century – based on fact – dark, violent.

Ripper Street – Netflix streaming – 5 seasons complete – 2012-2016
Matthew MacFadyen in a Jack the Ripper era London – dark, violent.

Vikings – Amazon Prime streaming – 6 seasons complete – 2013-2020
Violent tale of early culture where the women fight alongside the men.

Orphan Black – Amazon Prime streaming – 5 seasons complete – 2013-2017
Ultimate cloning with Tatania Maslany playing 8 parts with stunning differentiation – top-notch sci-fi.

Murdoch Mysteries – Acorn via Amazon Prime – 14 seasons – 2008-2021
Turn of the century Toronto with a science forward detective – light touch.

Miss Fisher's Murder Mysteries – Acorn via Amazon Prime – 3 seasons – 2012-2015 1920's Melbourne lady detective, costumes to die for – light touch.

The Good Wife"– Netflix DVD's only – 7 seasons complete – 2009-2015
Excellent from the Pilot on.

Madame Secretary – Netflix streaming – 6 seasons complete – 2014-2019
Tea Leoni as the CIA trained Secretary of State – well written.

Sleepy Hollow – Netflix DVDs only – 4 seasons – 2013-2017 Icabod Crane back from the dead to fight evil in modern day New York state – a hoot.

Parenthood – Netflix streaming – 6 seasons complete – 2010-2015 One of the best dramas about family relationships ever – deals with autism.

(Short series)

The Politician's Husband – Netflix streaming – 3 Episodes complete
David Tennant and Emily Watson in a British-style Borgen.

Happy Valley – Netflix streaming – 6 Episodes complete
Sarah Lancashire as a Yorkshire police Sergeant.

(Documentaries)

My Life As A Turkey – Netflix DVD One of the best!

(Movies)

Snowpiercer – Netflix streaming – A train with the last of the human race – unique sci-fi.

Flirting With Disaster – Netflix streaming Can't believe I never saw this 1996 David O. Russell comedy with Ben Stiller, Patricia Arquette, Tea Leoni, Richard Jenkins, Josh Brolin, Lily Tomlin, Alan Alda, Mary Tyler Moore, George Segal – absolutely a comic gem!

The Grand Seduction – Netflix streaming Taylor Kitsch and Brendan Gleeson in a comic delight about saving a fishing village in Nova Scotia.

Philomena – Netflix streaming Judi Dench as an Irish woman in search of her long lost child.

The Grand Budapest Hote – Netflix DVD Wes Anderson at his best.

The Angriest Man in Brooklyn – Netflix DVD One of Robin Williams last performances.

The Book Thief – Netflix DVD WWII story of a Jewish child kept by a foster family during Nazi occupation.

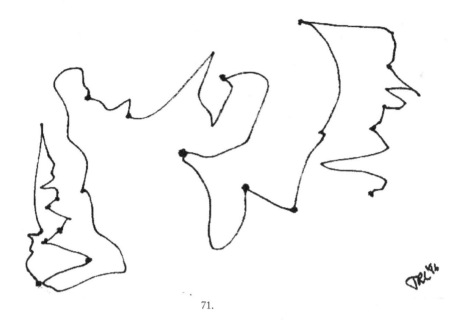

71.

2015 - Year Five

February 1
miracles

My brilliant therapist says the following is "by turns grateful, anguished, wondrous, angry, confused ..." That seems about right.

I have looked upon these emails as sacred acts. While undergoing crippling challenges in my life, they have kept me part of yours, and become my lifeline for an active support system of generous souls.

When last you heard, I was recovering from a successful hip replacement and gearing up for ankle surgery in February. On my last visit to the surgeon he witnessed my range of motion and said "I'm not sure we could get a better result than that". And this, after holding out a pipe dream of innovative repair for three years! My response is, instead of further surgery, to opt for magical thinking, since I am more mobile and pain-free than I had imagined possible. So far, I am upright much of the day and managing inside without the need for a cane. Just going with that, to see how far it gets me.

The challenge is to simply deal with what I find each day and try to make the most of it, while having to accept some deformity and disability.

I am happy to move away from the repair/recovery lifestyle, and now seek a physical balance that might heal itself well enough to enable me to rejoin friends and share worlds. So that's what I'm working on now. What I may need from you going forward is different, but not less.

It's a weird sort of a miracle!

When they ask "how did you heal your ankle", I will say "I shut myself away from the world for four years trusting the doctors might heal me and, after four repair surgeries, two of which worked, things finally just got better on their own". Stay tuned.

March 8
a live studio

Spent the month of February still homebound but able to move about inside without even needing a cane. What a dreary winter it has been! Not yet ready to tackle outdoors navigation, but in awe of those who have been trekking through it for way to long. This will be a most welcome spring.

At last I feel mobile enough to begin restructuring the studio, excavating archives and ideas. Mainly I have completed the first draft of the promised collection of emails you have received over the past four years. Working title: *Accidental Grit*. There is an introduction and an epilogue. The body of the work consists of the many carefully constructed email letters most of you have received from me over this long time. Upon re-reading the chronological weaving of the tale, I am reminded of how much I owe to so many for helping bring me through this strange and often awkward journey.

I begin this 5th year of post-traumatic existence with high hopes and a full heart.

May 1
mayday

Much healing has taken place since the hip replacement last July. I am able to move around my apartment relatively easily. Some tasks seem more and more possible – like cooking meals, writing and organizing in the studio, even taking short accompanied walks with a friend. But too much walking and I'm immobile the next day. This body, having undergone violent injury and resultant incapacity, hoping for years to regain full mobility, now fails to support me. I struggle with reworking my soul to fit into this new body. I always felt lucky I had a fortunate body, a body that heals well, a body that would help me age gracefully, so I could dance the rest of my life. Well, the grace is gone. I don't know whose body this is. It seems connected to me in some way, but requires different interactions. Bigger clothes, for instance. I suspect more surgery will be called for, meaning more hospitalization, more recovery. I will continue to need your support for some time to come.

May 19
call to alms

I try to communicate a positive turn of events, but the truth is this whole upset in my life required funds I did not have. With donations from many of you and my small social security I have been able to survive, but four years on, there are large purchases necessary (new window air conditioner and upcoming summer Con Ed bill, new prescription glasses, essential dental work, lease renewal, increased transportation needs, and the ongoing need for help with housekeeping and body work not covered by Medicare or Medicaid).

I seem to be putting the days/weeks/months together, but after this long time of being less than able-bodied, the reserves are running out. Only give as you are able, but if you can, please offer me a bit of a lifeline for a while longer.

July 5
cultivating independence

Still here due to the generosity from many good people who have responded to my plight over these more than four years. Special thanks to all who recently donated to The Corporeal Studio, Ltd.

Making the effort to get out close to home, but the ankle is not durable. Up on it too long and it refuses to hold. I am facing the acceptance of a 'disabled' label, having lived with the fantasy for so long that full lmobility would at some time be possible. Still investigating further surgical intervention, but also taking the days as they come and doing the best I can. I'm out of the house but not out of the neighborhood, still very far from returning to an active life. At the age of 72, after years of some very tough survival challenges, I think I finally know what it takes to cultivate friendship. This dance we do with life has become my 8th decade project.

With love and admiration for all you do, all you endure, and all you enjoy,

October 12
life in the slow lane

Happy to report I am now able to take care of simple pedestrian errands a few blocks from home and was recently certified for Access-a-Ride, a reasonably priced alternative to costly car services. Joining the disabled community reminds me how many New Yorkers are dependent on public services in order to make it to necessary appointments. Unfortunately I have been left waiting in the street for over an hour each time I've used it, so I've written to Mayor DeBlasio in hopes he will be interested in improving this much needed service for those of us who need help in travel.

Having crawled back to some sort of life after years of hiding inside with pain and confusion, I realize there are new bottom-line needs. I can no longer do my own large grocery shopping or full scale house cleaning or laundry. For these things I rely on paid help pushing the fixed social security budget out of whack.

My body has responded to a summer of eating well, having nearly lost the 20 pounds I gained, and before getting out of bed every morning I do at least 45 minutes of exercise addressing all the joints and applying quality physical therapy absorbed over many years. I manage the stairs nearly every day to get the mail and get out into the lovely summer/fall weather. Walking outside is a challenging meditation – each step mindfully weighed as to the angle of the sidewalk, the obstacles both pedestrian and vehicular, and the relative stability of the foot on the pavement, the positioning of the cane, the balance. I never believed I could be so focused, but, since hurrying is out of the question, slow moving is my new reality.

After deciding against further surgery and leaving the medical options behind, I faced huge doubts about 'what is work' and 'what next'? Writing to you these many years has brought out part of the story, but I recently began to address it in a simple narrative.
In the re-telling of what happened to me I am dealing with a lot of accumulated PTSD – letting it go, bit by bit.

Thank you for your recent donations and good wishes. Acknowledgement letters from Corporeal will reach you by the end of the year. I fear, however, I may be among the needy for some time to come.

With your continued help and my increasing ability to maintain a strong focus, I begin this fifth autumn season since the accident, full of hope.

November 29
more than thanks

As we close Thanksgiving week and enter into Christmas madness, I just want you to know how much I appreciate your presence in my life and all the individual kindnesses you have sent my way during these nearly five years of incapacity and insecurity. You inspire me, encourage me to be my best self. Even while mostly alone, thoughts of you cut into my solitude and remind me how lucky I am to have friends who care.

Through all of you, I have learned to lead with gratitude, function through acceptance, and ask for help when needed.

We present to others our chosen mask – a panacea for failure to see clear truth beyond our own perception. Our masked self becomes the instrument of our choices, the material of our actions, the result of harsh or kind influences that have touched us. If we have been abused or suffered deeply, the mask hardens. Only those who look beneath the mask can bring a softening, to reveal brief glimmers of truth shared.

Please accept the grace of my blessing on your lives and may you continue to thrive in a troublesome world rife with fear and uncertainty.

PART IV - AFTERMATH

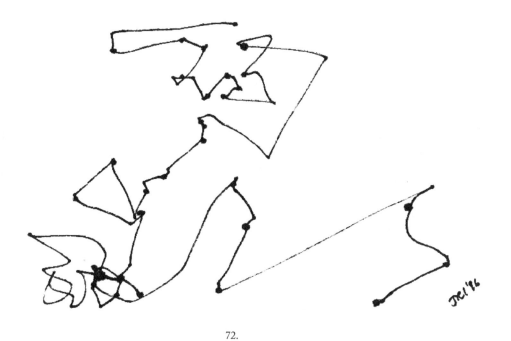

72.

January 1
processing life

> change is happening
> advantage is perspective
> choice is given
> truth is elusive
> peace is within
> joy is dissociative
> bliss is silent
> survival is obvious
> sorrow is constant
> struggle is limiting
> health is elusive
> pain is unavoidable
> presence is required
> people are traps
> masses are stupid
> rulers are selfish
> systems are prejudiced
> movements are threatening
> ideas are dangerous
> individuals rule
> absence degenerates
> awareness begs
> resistance fails
> aggression destroys
> submission erases
> despair obliterates
> life becomes death
>
> process is everything.

February 2
no more doctors

The long period of medical crisis, hospitalization, intervention and dependency has abated. As of this writing I'm still largely homebound, but mobile enough to get around my apartment relatively pain-free, able to function with some degree of normalcy. I have not yet tackled the world, but having suspended a long reliance on what doctor's think, and instead accepted the fact that I go forward deformed and disabled with a medically non-viable ankle.

This is my final communique with the ankle doctor:

Dear Dr. Sheskier,

I sent this earlier in July and was informed you were unavailable until August 3rd, so reaching out again.

I had to take a break from all doctors for a while. Tried relying on fortitude, grit and my own physical therapy for nearly 6 months. Trial period revealed that unless this ankle is repaired in some way, the rest of the leg is at risk for further deterioration. I have little mobility over the long run. Not what I had hoped for when first consulting you, after a year's delay, to finally see you in January of 2012.

The disappointment in waiting 3 years for your promises of a 'miraculous' ankle replacement took a great toll. I had to regroup and figure out what I could do on my own. At this juncture I am reasonably functional indoors, but without endurance. Recently tested it with a long walk and the result was additional pain in the knee. I fear the lower leg bones are taking the brunt of weight-bearing since the talus is missing.

I last saw you in January 2015 and then went for a CT Scan. I have not had a follow-up appointment since that time. I don't like leaving our association with so much frustration and confusion. I know you want to help me and, in good faith, have tried, but circumstances were seemingly not favorable and time wore on and on. Let me know what might be our best next move.

Thank you,
Judith Ren-Lay

241

The ensuing last visit with this ankle specialist offered this: "You shouldn't be able to stand up on that ankle, much less walk". So I decided this was as far as I could go with his help.

The plan was to get back into life in ways I could discover as I entered the 5th year of post traumatic coping. Writing it all down continued to be a healing act.

February 14
valentine of sharing

So much of life comes down to walking – the ambulatory response to situations and circumstances. When that is removed, or challenged, our choices are thrown into a state of dependency and inner chaos. Weathering this maelstrom of what is perceived as failure, is the greatest barrier to moving on.

Gone are the days when I take my body for granted. As I walked today the 7 blocks to and from the bank on Broadway, I encountered people who are not thinking about their body. They roller blade and saunter, weave and turn about sharply with seemingly little thought of where they are in space, where their foot may fall, how they will balance the change of forces impacting their moves. I can't even remember what that felt like. If I don't gingerly, slowly, consciously adjust to putting one foot down and then the next, I am unable to function in the world of action. This is a change no one tells you about when you are challenged with age or disability. It isn't so much the physical exertion, because I always feel great after I accomplish this simple activity in the world, it is the mental focus required. I experience a sort of wholeness of mind and body, accepting the slow and careful approach as necessary. I wonder there aren't more mishaps and accidents around me as I witness a kind of casual foolhardiness where minds seem always to be somewhere else – spinning with anticipation of what is to come, engrossed in their conversations, glued to their phones, no longer finding meaning in what is happening around them, but always in an altered state of pretending to be already in the future or at least headed in that direction.

After relying for five years on the flowing kindness of many, I am now largely on my own and find myself not so kind to me as others have been. I sense a growing desperation. Occasionally there is a glimmer of purpose and resolve, but then the bottom drops out and I am falling into old age, unprotected and alone. Some say I think too much. Perhaps. But this contemplation of the trajectory of one's life has been the work of mine, and refuses to stop. So I retreat from fretting and enter into fantasies of what I would still like to have, to be, to do. Then find myself a bit clueless as to how to make the fantasies true, in order to rejoin the world once again.

I have to face the very real fact that current capacity for movement is as good as it's going to get. In spite of the carefully constructed work-arounds bringing myself to this level of mobility, there are so many things I will never be able to do again, walking very far at a reasonable pace being the most crushing, but also managing stairs, standing too long, expanded travel, dancing with abandon, climbing a ladder.

In the years after my accident I learned how to rein in time, satisfy present reality, keep each passing moment relatively free from fear or dread, and get by on the day to day. Last spring and summer I began to get out of the house, but since the shattered ankle was never repaired, it only holds me up for short periods of time.

Meantime I continue to write with a book in mind, a chronicle of these past five years of post-accident encounters with truth and survival.

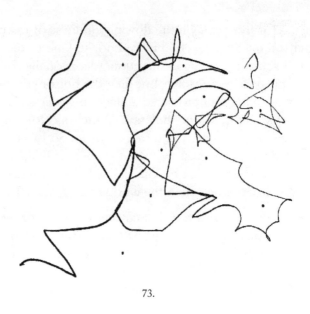

73.

EPILOGUE

Ten years on, my awareness of time keeps changing.

The clock rules momentary time, this time, the present time, as I keep trying to engage, in the remainder of my life, choices that may make a difference. Each day there is more to accomplish than there is time to do it, so I set aside all but the basics, the essential tasks that keep me going for as long as I have left. That includes eating for both health and pleasure, managing household help and shopping, grooming and providing presentational choices, so when I dress I feel good about my image in the mirror. I exercise just enough to remain pain free, never seeming to make headway in improving my fitness and conditioning. I seem always just barely functional, with daily sneezing fits, ongoing difficulty walking and breathing a challenge. For so many years my body was all that was really important. Now my enjoyment of life, such as it is, takes precedence over an unrelenting drive to train. I relent, give in, give up somewhat and spend more time sitting at the computer and watching video drama than I spend exercising.

Too aware of the total span of my life I try to make sense of it in language, still writing consistently my reflections, my take on the whole thing such as it is.

The arc of a day presents choices from awakening, rising, breaking the fast and attending to whatever work I see before me to do. I feed on getting in mail, both snail and e, attending to any scheduled appointments, taking in as much news as I can handle these days. I am always a bit relieved when it seems to be time to go to bed and try to sleep. I have great difficulty with sleeping, often stay up until 5am, then sleep the rest of the morning to make sure I get in at least 8 hours. I have learned to never schedule anything before 2pm, and 3pm is often preferable.

On a weekly basis, I have learned to only schedule going into the world every other day. Each outing takes so much out of me, I need at least a day to recover before I face emerging again. This means I spend a lot of time without showering or washing my hair, often in my pajamas. I learned from so much hospital time that I do just fine with the occasional 'Huggies' shower and can wash my hair in the sink. If I have to attend an event that is important, it often takes me more than 2 hours to prepare, needing to have all details covered before I venture into what feels like the unknown. I have not traveled for 8 years. The prospect of carrying luggage or facing the walking required is daunting and I fear my ankle will totally give out on me and I will be in the world alone unable to function. I deeply miss experiences in natural settings, but remember my retreat times at Ocean Grove and those blessed weeks house-sitting for Dona and Brad in Vermont and find sense-memory really does work.

Seasons pass and I make an effort to provide a comfortable environment by responding to temperature changes. In fact this little survival capsule has been customized over the years to make going anywhere else a sacrifice of comfort. At this stage of life all I really want is to be comfortable and when I try to stretch out and expand my influence and presence, it is often too much to bear. This rent-stabilized apartment, my living installation, brings me pleasure satisfying most corporeal needs. Here I have the tools to continue to write, the exercise space and toys, and the kitchen and bathroom and sleeping requirements firmly met. To try to exist somewhere else would mean giving up the hard won comfort I have created here over the last 40 years and maintain through the grace of social security and friends.

Each year, each birthday takes me by surprise. "How did that happen?" I always ask. Since the accident I have great difficulty garnering the motivation to continue to do anything the rest of the world deems worthwhile. As to performing again, I would love the opportunity, but my meager efforts in this direction face me with the stupidity of competition, as I see an entirely new aesthetic has replaced what I am about. To lobby for support has proven an empty gesture towards giving the world too much power over the rest of my life. And it no longer seems worth the effort, bringing more frustration and stress than satisfaction. I no longer engage with my work the way I once could. I begin to see a futility in continuing to believe I have anything of value to offer a world that seems to be careening toward an under-valuing of language, a growing support for those who have already made names for themselves, and a tendency to ignore those who have aged, largely unknown. The very basis of communication has morphed into phone to phone texting, emojis and memes, the occasional on-line chat and social media. I can't seem to keep up with these changes, and part of me doesn't want to.

As to the life I have lived, in contemplation of leaving this world, I am aware end of life issues must be faced, but put off making a will, fearing making a post-life plan will put the period at the end of the sentence too soon. Longevity is my genetic heritage, but unless I catch a break, I will grow old in poverty.

I periodically sort through my archives and marvel at the 40 plus years of work I have produced, the many wonderful artists with whom I have been fortunate enough to collaborate over those years, and often feel quite validated. Going forward, for as long as I am able, I continue to offer these books, also stories, poems, and the occasional music/song performance.

Judith Ren-Lay
New York City
June 2022

74. COMEDY (24x14 ink on paper) j.r-l.

INDEX
PHOTOGRAPHS AND ILLUSTRATIONS
(in order of appearance)

CPSIA information can be obtained
at www.ICGtesting.com
Printed in the USA
LVHW110858121222
735009LV00002B/11